THE BOOK OF RUTH LINE BY LINE

J. DARLINE PEIPMAN

The Book of Ruth Line by Line
by J. Darline Peipman

Printed in the United States of America

ISBN 1-594678-78-2

All Bible quotations are taken from the King James Version of the Bible.

www.xulonpress.com

Dedication

It is with love that I gratefully dedicate this book to four women who have meant so very much to me.

To my dear Mother, Elsie Mae Luff Roesch – Many times I saw her late at night reading the Bible. She taught me to reverence the Word of God. As a child of four, I knelt at her knee to give my life to the Lord.

To the memory of my dear friend Amy Culver Terry – She and her husband introduced me to my husband because they were sure God meant us for each other. They prayed for us daily over the years. She encouraged me to write this book and hoped to be able to read it before she went Home. There is no longer any need for her to read about Ruth since I am sure she has already met Ruth.

To a beautifully spiritual lady Carolyn Shuler – She never misses an opportunity to share a Scripture or several. Her love of the Lord is always evident in every conversation and letter. She is an inspiration.

To the memory of my dear mother-in-law, Hilda Helene Kents Peipman – She taught me what a mother-in-law should be by her loving example. I had to go to the other side of the world to meet her but she accepted this foreigner with open arms and heart.

Acknowledgements

All quotations are from the King James Version of the Bible. The scholarly and very godly men who worked on the translation did not use the English of their day. They went back to the English used some one hundred years before to enable them to give a true and accurate translation of the Hebrew. Since the book of Ruth borders on being poetry it is even more important to have accuracy of translation. (Poetry says so much in so few words.) It is with grateful acknowledgement of their tremendous dedication to the task of bringing God's Word to all readers of the English language that we must be eternally grateful.

I am also grateful to those who over the years have compiled concordances, lexicons, and dictionaries.

It is with thankfulness and gratitude that I acknowledge the kind (or as Ruth would say in Hebrew, checed) support of especially my husband Fred and our grown children, Kathryn (Kate), Nathaniel (Nate), Andrew, Aimee, and Lydia. They are God's blessing to me.

Table of Contents

Preface

Several years ago, I decided to try and memorize the book of Ruth. As the words were repeated over and over in my mind, they took on more clarity with deeper meaning than ever before and that was pure joy.

In looking at Ruth's story, line by line, I tried to understand the great working of God in the lives of Ruth, Boaz, Naomi, and the others in the story. It became important to try and comprehend how they understood God. In searching out the way words were used in other Scriptures, I therefore limited my use to only those Scriptures that came before the time of Ruth and would have been available to them. (There were some exceptions using quotes from the Psalms.) I did this because the people in the book of Ruth would have been limited to understanding God through their own experience and only the Scriptures they had by this time period.

Ruth's story is the story of ordinary individuals living out their ordinary lives. And what is so very extraordinary is that their story becomes living Scripture. It seems extraordinary that the life of an ordinary human being could become a part of the Word of God. Slowly, over many centuries, and painstakingly with insightful detail, God writes the history of earth and the meaning of life through the deeds and lives of many people but primarily through the lives of His faithful followers, those who place their trust in Him.

The book of Ruth is given to us, as is the entire Bible, for instruction and guidance in the way we should live our lives in relationship to Him and others. In the Bible there is a unity of thought revealing the mind of God. God reveals Himself through His Word. We come to appreciate that every word has not only meaning but also deep significance. We are promised that not one word shall pass away or be lost. If it is that important to God, for each word to be saved, then not one word is an idle word. Should we not then consider each word carefully?

Biblical word study is ecstatically exhilarating. Beyond simple meaning there are shades of meaning and subtleties of meaning. That exciting eureka moment of revelation is the high point of understanding what the words are telling us. The words then have deep significance for and in our lives.

We will take a closer look at the expanded meaning of some of the key words by looking at the fuller Hebrew definitions. This gives not only a broader but also a deeper understanding of what the text is telling us.

In this book, each verse is consecutively studied. The verse is given and then examined by individual words or phrases listed as headings in bold type.

In looking at the book of Ruth line by line and sometimes, word by word, we see the Word magnified. Looking through a magnifying glass does not change the object viewed. The object remains the same. What does change is our perception. We see more clearly, with greater definition. It is my hope and prayer that this book will magnify the LORD.

J. Darline Peipman
Westhampton, NY, November, 2004

Chapter One

Many, many years ago, in the homes of the privileged and well to do of England and France, socially prominent hostesses would hold what was referred to as "drawing rooms." Guests would arrive in their finest evening dress expecting to find a new and novel entertainment. It might be a musical evening to hear the latest composition of a well-known composer or the work of a composer as yet unknown but highly promising. The "drawing room" might also be a literary evening with someone such as Lord Byron reading his latest poem.

On one such evening, a courtly older foreign gentleman had a story (not his own) to tell to the assembled guests. He said he would change the names of the main characters to protect their identity. As gossip and the latest scandalous stories were always avidly pounced upon, he soon had everyone's rapt attention.

They listened to his every word to see if they could figure out of whom he was speaking. As he told the story, they were moved, sometimes to tears. It was so romantic. The craftsmanship was exquisite and the suspense kept them wondering about the outcome to the very end.

After listening to the story the excited and delighted guests declared it perfection and demanded to know the name of the author of this incredible creation. They exclaimed over its lyrical qualities. It was a brilliant work of art. They again pleaded to know who this new author was and if he had written any more such stories. He would be in much demand. Where could they get a copy of his book? Who was he?

In the crowded fashionably elegant drawing room, Benjamin Franklin gave a slight bow of acquiescence. His audience hushed.

With a slight smile and a merry twinkle in his eyes he said, "My friends, you have not read your Bible. There you will find the story of Ruth."

The book of Ruth is indeed an artistically exquisite story. It is a delight. It is not only a romance with an element of suspense, it is also the story of ordinary people who lived and found true happiness. In many ways it could be our story. From times now shrouded in dusty antiquity these people come to us once again as we see them in full color through the individual words and phrases of this ancient text. Let us begin.

Part One – The Move to Moab
Ruth 1:1 to Ruth 1:5

> *Ruth 1:1 "Now it came to pass in the days when the judges ruled, that there was a famine in the land. And a certain man of Bethlehem-judah went to sojourn in the country of Moab, he, and his wife, and his two sons."*

Now

Now is a very arresting word. It is a STOP, and take notice, word. Now gives us the feeling that everything that has happened in the past has led up to this point in time. *Now* is also a point from which we start. From this very spot, centuries and millenniums ago, we will be spectators of what takes place. It is as if this story, the book of Ruth, was unfolding before our very eyes. A lot has already occurred that led up to this moment in time but *NOW* we will see and hear what happens next.

As the first word of the book of Ruth, *now* is significant.

Only nine of the sixty-six books of the Bible start with the word now and all of these are in the Old Testament. Six of the nine books' opening verses also contain the phrase – it came to pass. (Joshua, Judges, Esther, II Samuel, Ruth and Ezekiel)

Now is a marker on God's time line. Something of very special importance is going to happen. The significant *now* events in the other five books (besides the book of Ruth) mentioned above are as follows:

Joshua	-	The Lord speaks to Joshua telling him to lead His people
Judges	-	The children of Israel ask the Lord for a leader and He answered
II Samuel	-	David is promised the eternal throne
Esther	-	The Israelite people are saved from genocide
Ezekiel	-	The heavens opened and Ezekiel sees a vision of God

All of these events were historic markers on God's time line of His plans for His people. The *now* moment that begins the book of Ruth is an extremely important and significant moment. God is intervening for a very special reason. It will affect the life, of not just one person, not only a family, not only a nation, but it will change the lives of every one of us.

It

Now *it* came to pass. "*It*" is a pronoun so we have to ask, what does *it* represent? Being the second word in the text gives *it* strong significance. At first glance, *it* seems to represent the famine and a man's response to this situation.

It, however, is more than an event (famine) and a decision (to move). *It* has to do with something much larger and grander. On the surface, the scene seems rather ordinary, perhaps even insignificant but because of the intervention of God, the ordinary becomes very significant.

With millions upon millions of cameras, we try to capture "the moment." There are books about one day in the life of . . .. We find it fascinating to talk about, "What were you doing when . . .?" Somehow we know that our place in that event has significance. Somehow we know intuitively that our every action and reaction is profoundly significant. If only we could record the moments and see them as a part of the grander scheme.

The pronoun *it,* here in the book of Ruth is the hand of God. *It* is the movement of God in history, in a particular place at a particular time. *It* is the continuing working out of God's plan for a people, for a nation, and for all the generations of the world to come. *It* is shrouded in the eternal mystery of the great I AM. And although we see through a glass darkly, one thing is clear. *It came.*

Came

Came indicates that there is a history that took place before this Kodak cameo time frame and it has all rolled forward, totally unimpeded, to this very spot. We have a feeling that there were events just waiting to happen. Like a giant locomotive coming down the track, it turned neither to the left nor to the right, never jumped the track and nothing could stop it or stand in its way. In a headlong hurtle of power it reaches this point. *Now it came.*

Going back some thousand years before Ruth, we have Abraham called to be the father of the nation of Israel. Between the times of Abraham, until the time of the book of

Ruth the Bible gives an account of the nation of Israel and God's dealings with her. The book of Ruth is a pivotal point in this narrative. *Now it came.* The quiet, gentle, exquisitely written book of Ruth and indeed the life of Ruth mark the change in Old Testament focus. At the end of the book, the birth of David, who would become king of Israel, is announced and for about the next thousand years of Biblical narrative, the Old Testament centers on the kingdom and the coming King of Kings.

To Pass

Now it came *to pass.* In this instance, *to pass* does not mean something that has gone by, as in, "The car passed mine as if I were standing still." A closer meaning would be expressed in, "Please pass the butter," that is, the butter is going by other people to get to me. Many events in the lives of many people led up to this point (the time of Ruth.) The effect of these previous events is seen in the history of this one family, so long ago.

There are many examples in the Bible in which this passing of time is allowed until "the fullness of time." There are many small decisions and events, which occur before a culminating event occurs. We do not, we cannot examine all that took place before the book of Ruth but we focus on a particular time – a real time – a particular people – real people – and observe.

In

In is a focusing word. We even say, "in focus." We are going to focus and take a close look at people and events, decisions made, and how these decisions affect lives far into the future. There is something very profound to be learned, of epic proportions, even though the immediate scene looks very pastoral, rural, bucolic, and peaceful. We become aware that the seemingly insignificant decisions of daily life can have effects generations later. All of life becomes clearly and vastly significant as we look at and focus on the simple life of one guileless, innocent, foreign girl in the panorama of history.

In gives the awareness of being surrounded by other events, which is indeed the case. On a national level the book of Judges describes what is happening in the nation of Israel. Armies march and counter march across the country. There are scenes of savagery, lawlessness, and lust. Israel is defeated and ground under the heel of her oppressor. Israel cries to God for freedom. Great godly leaders come to power. They play their part, the day is won, the people return to the worship of God. But, the leader eventually passes on and again the people forget God and again there are scenes of desolation and strife.

In the middle of this clash of arms and tumult of war, is set the almost serene, romantic, pastoral, and lovely story of Ruth. Here we have the life of ordinary people who actually lived in this time period.

Men and nations rise and fall. Battles are fought; some won, some lost. There are political intrigues and rivalries and treachery in high places. There is great unrest and uncertainty. Yet the life of the people went on as it had done for ages past and it would do for ages to come. There were still crops to plant and the customs and holidays to be observed. There was love and marriage and children to care for. There was the simple faith in the goodness of God. This simple ongoing life of the common people is the focus of the scene for the book of Ruth even though the backdrop is a picture of cruelty and bloodshed depicted in the book of Judges.

The Days

Yowm (alternate spelling yom) is the Hebrew word used here for day. It is an important word and is used well over two thousand times in the Old Testament. The word can mean a day, several days, a period of time, a year, and a lifetime such as "in his day". It can also mean daytime since regular hours were not marked, but rather, regulated by natural phenomena (the sun going down.) In fact, a day that we mark into twenty-four- hour periods starting at midnight, for the Israelites started at sundown. In America, standardized time was a matter of local preference until the advent of the railroad when schedules became important for switching tracks and avoiding accidents.

Yowm is connected with the sovereignty of God. He existed before time began. God created time and it is under His control. God is very interested in time and human events. Our days are numbered and we are to redeem the time He has allotted to each of us. Each day counts. When we come across the expression "the day when" introducing events in the Bible, those events have particular importance in the history of salvation.

When The Judges Ruled

After the death of Moses, who led the Israelites out of Egypt and to the border of the Promised Land, God called Joshua to be their military leader. Joshua would lead the people into battles for the conquest and settlement of the Promised Land. They had to do battle but God promised the victory.

The children of Israel were on the threshold of a brighter future than almost any people in the history of the whole world. It was second only to the future that lay before Adam and Eve (until the Fall) and Noah and his family (after the flood.) Theirs' would be a life filled with great richness. Their forefathers had been slaves, beaten and abused, on the whim of viciously cruel taskmasters. For centuries these descendants of Abraham (by now possibly a couple of million people) had been waiting for this golden moment.

The promise had been passed down, generation after generation. It was never, never forgotten. The belief in the promise could not be mocked or jeered or beaten out of them. The order by the Pharaoh of Egypt to kill their precious infant sons only made them long for the day when they would enter into the land of so great a promise. God had promised the land of Canaan to their father Abraham. God renewed the covenant promise with Abraham's son Isaac and had renewed it again with Isaac's son Jacob. Abraham believed in all that God had promised him and God counted his belief as righteousness.

The time had finally come. The land of great promise was literally in view. There on the border, sections of the land are allotted to each tribe (family groups that descended from the twelve sons of Jacob.) Interestingly, they divided up the land before it was even possessed. They divided it in faith that it would, with God's help, be theirs.

The fighting for conquest in order to settle the land began. And after many great battles under the leadership of Joshua, starting with Jericho, Joshua dies; he dies before the land can be fully won. What now? After the death of Joshua, the people asked God about who would lead them.

> "Now after the death of Joshua it came to pass, that the children of Israel asked the LORD, saying, Who shall go up for us against the Canaanites first, to fight against them?" Judges 1:1

God tells them that the tribe of Judah will lead them and eventually much more of the land is conquered. (But, to this day, not all of the land has ever been fully possessed. See Deuteronomy 11:24 and Joshua 1:3 and 4.)

The people served God during Joshua's lifetime and even after his death. They served God as long as the elders lived who had seen all the great works of the Lord that He did for Israel. (Judges 2:7). The next generation, however, did not serve the Lord. They did evil.

> "And they forsook the LORD God of their fathers, which brought them out of the land of Egypt, and followed other gods, of the gods of the people that were round about them, and bowed themselves unto them, and provoked the LORD to anger." Judges 2:12

In one generation, Israel forgot all that the Lord had done for them. They fell into grave sin. It made the Lord angry.

> "And the anger of the Lord was hot against Israel, and he delivered them into the hands of the spoilers…" Judges 2:14a

> "Nevertheless the Lord raised up judges, which delivered them out of the hand of those who spoiled them," Judges 2:16

The book of Judges is a record of twelve men and one woman who were raised up, by God, to deliver Israel from their enemies. The book of Judges in Hebrew is called Shophetim. Interestingly, 1000 years later the Phoenicians used a similar word, suffetes, which means magistrate. In the Samaritan record the judges are called "kings." In the Hebrew Bible, Judges is the second book of the "Former

Prophets." A judge then was a person who had divine authority having been raised up by God. He was a prophet, that is, spoke the word of God and was a military as well as political leader in the sense that he was raised up to deliver Israel from her enemies.

This time was one of the darkest in Israel's history. This pattern of falling away and suffering the consequences, was followed by repenting and crying out to the Lord. Then He mercifully rescued them. This was repeated time and again for several centuries. Over and over there was this repetition of rebellion, retribution, repentance, and restoration. During this period, enemy armies overran the land. They plundered and stole. Horrors were committed against the people of Israel. Sometimes, after that, they were even taken into slavery.

And so it was, during this time period in which the story of Ruth takes place; *when the judges ruled.*

That There Was A Famine In The Land

There was a famine in the Promised Land, the land that was promised to be flowing with milk and honey. How could this be? The Hebrew word for famine is raab and could also be translated hunger. There was a time of hunger in the land. This was not the first time *that there was a famine in the land.*

Many years before, the Lord directed Abraham to leave Ur, at the time a modern city and a culture of high sophistication. And he did leave. He set out on his journey, to destination unknown and towards an uncertain future, to a place where God would show him. He travels many miles. Eventually, (skipping a lot of interesting details) he stops for a while in Canaan and then, *there was a famine in the land.*

No one would wonder if, at this point, we were told that

Abraham has a crisis of faith. "Did I really hear from God?" God tells him to move to this place and then he was stuck in the middle of hard times. But we are not told that Abraham wavered in his faith for even a moment. He decides to go to Egypt.

Abraham realizes that he has a very beautiful wife (even though at this point she is already sixty-five!) He fears that he might be killed so that some other man might have her. As a precautionary measure, he asks her to say she is his sister. Sarah's beauty is soon noted and Pharaoh, the king of Egypt, is made aware of this beautiful lady. Sarah is taken into the house of the Pharaoh. Pharaoh has decided to make Sarah his wife.

At this point it would be fair to ask why Sarah continued to keep going along with this whole charade. What compelled her? Why did she do it? What would make any woman do it?

Perhaps, in some ways, the decision was simple. She had made a covenant vow, a vow that is hardly understood today. She was truly married and one with Abraham. She had given herself in totality. She trusted in the vow she made before God. She trusted God through Abraham with her entire life. And God is faithful. He would not disappoint her trust.

And so the story continues. In those days, in Egypt, there were weeks of preparation in bathing and skin treatments with oils and so forth before a woman could come to her new husband. During this time, Abraham is treated generously because of his "sister" and given sheep and oxen and camels and maidservants and menservants. He was given royal bounty in a big way. Everyone is thinking what a lucky man he is and Abraham must have been wondering, "Now what am I going to do?" The situation looks pretty grim.

Then a strange thing happens. The house of Pharaoh is hit with one disaster after another. Pharaoh knows exactly what the problem is and he confronts Abraham (who at that time was still named Abram and Sarah was still Sarai. (God changed their names later.)

> "And Pharaoh called Abram, and said, What is this that thou hast done unto me? Why didst thou not tell me that she was thy wife? Why saidst thou, She is my sister? so I might have taken her to me to wife; now therefore behold thy wife, take her, and go thy way. And Pharaoh commanded his men concerning him: and they sent him away, and his wife, and all that he had." Genesis. 12:18-20

It is not too difficult to imagine the anger in Pharaoh's voice. Abraham and Sarah were fortunate to leave without severe retribution. Pharaoh knew, however, that if God had caused disasters because of his innocent intent to marry Sarah, what would happen if he laid even a finger on them? Even so, Pharaoh did hustle them out of there and with an escort to make sure they left promptly. He did not even want anything back that he had given Abraham. He just wanted them gone.

So the hand of God rescues Sarah and Abraham from a dangerous situation that they had brought upon themselves and in His loving watch-care they are even better off than before. Abraham was a very rich man.

Years later, Abraham's son Isaac faces famine in Canaan and went to stay in Gerar in the land of the Philistines. Isaac's son Jacob and his family also face widespread famine. But God had already spoken to the Pharaoh of Egypt in a dream. Because Joseph, the son of Jacob, was able to tell Pharaoh what the dream meant (that seven years of famine were coming), Pharaoh put Joseph in charge of preparing the country for famine. He was made second in command of the country. He was second only to Pharaoh. When the famine came it was very widespread and, ultimately, it caused all of Jacob's family to move to Egypt where Jacob's son Joseph had prepared the country with enough food to see the country through the difficult time. The Lord truly had Joseph in the right place at the right time. The family continued there for four hundred years until led out by Moses.

Why were there these periods of famine in the land of Canaan as seen in Genesis and here in the book of Ruth? While the Israelites were in the wilderness, the Lord spoke to them about the blessings that would pour down upon them if Israel would but obey Him. He also warned them about the punishment if they did not obey Him.

> "And I will break the pride of your power; and I will make your heaven as iron, and your earth as brass: And your strength shall be spent in vain: for your land shall not yield her increase, neither shall the trees of the land, yield their fruits." Leviticus 26:19 and 20

> "And thy heaven that is over thy head shall be brass, and the earth that is under thee shall be iron. The LORD shall make the rain of thy land powder and dust: from heaven shall it come down upon thee, until thou be destroyed." Deuteronomy 28:23 and 24

As well as the lack of rainfall and the resultant crop failure, famine can also be caused by pestilence. In addition, it can also be caused by pillage and marauding of marching armies feeding the troops with the food belonging to the local people. The time of the judges, in which the book of Ruth is set, is a time of intermittent warfare and then periods of peace when the people repented of their disobedience. We are not told what caused the famine, only *that there was a famine,* in the land of Israel.

And A Certain Man

In stating *a certain man,* we are told that not all of the families in the town, or even a large number of families, or even several families, decided to move. We can see that the spotlight is very focused. It is focused on one man. God is focusing, as He often does, on the life of the individual. We are seeing from God's perspective. He is intimately concerned with the individual. Of all the millions of people in the world we are focused on this one man.

Of Bethlehem-Judah

Bethlehem (the setting for this book) was located in the part of the Promised Land allotted to the tribe of Judah. There was another town by the name of Bethlehem but it was in the land allotted to the tribe of Zebulon. In order to distinguish between the two, the name of the town was followed by its location among the tribes such as we distinguish Bridgeport, Connecticut from Bridgeport, West Virginia by using the state name. Bethlehem in Judah is some six miles south of Jerusalem. Bethlehem literally means house of bread.

The first mention of Bethlehem in the Bible goes all the way back to Genesis 35:19. Jacob had fallen in love with Rachel practically from the moment that he first saw her. He struck up a bargain with her father to work for him for seven years in order to have her hand bestowed upon him. Her father tricked Jacob on the wedding night by giving Jacob

Rachel's sister Leah. Jacob then agreed to work another seven years and finally wins his beloved Rachel.

Skipping ahead in the story to when Rachel is expecting their second child, the family is once more moving and on the way, Rachel goes into labor. It is a difficult labor and as the baby is born, with Jacob by her side, Rachel dies. Jacob buries her in Ephrath. (Years later, sometime after the conquest, Ephrath is renamed Bethlehem.) Jacob sets up a pillar there on her grave, which stayed there for hundreds of years. When Jacob is old and near death himself and far away in Egypt his mind goes back to his beautiful Rachel and to Bethlehem where he left a part of his heart.

Went

In Hebrew, the word for went (the verb to go) is yalak. The word is used thirteen times in the book of Ruth. The number thirteen is often associated with rebellion. The book of Ruth does not mention rebellion. It does not contain any overt condemnation, accusation, or judgment. There is no assessment of any action taken. (The only exception being Naomi's assessment of her own situation, which will be discussed when we come to it.) The action, in the story, is simply reported. We are free to make up our own minds, make our own assessments, and to learn from the lives of these people. The concept here of going (*went*) is very important. It will have a profound effect on the story.

It is significant that we are told that this man *went* before we actually find out who he is. Will the going affect the characters for better or for worse? What must be considered is the direction in which the going takes them. Does it take them towards God or away from Him? The events that follow must speak for themselves.

To Sojourn

This certain man went to *sojourn,* to stay awhile. This was not to be a permanent move. He did not plan on living there forever. We have to wonder if this was or was not God's perfect plan for his life. There was a Biblical precedent for moving away from famine into a nearby land that was not affected by famine. We have seen that Abraham went to Egypt, Isaac went to Gerar in the land of the Philistines, and Jacob went to Egypt.

In the case of Abraham, God told him to go. In the case of Isaac, God told him to go. In the case of Jacob, God had allowed Jacob's son Joseph to prepare provision for them and all of Egypt during the years of famine. Was this certain man's sojourn, as related here in the book of Ruth, how God was going to save this man's life?

Once Israel had entered the Promised Land, they were to stay there and not live elsewhere. The land had been apportioned and had to stay in the family forever. It could not be sold.

It is now centuries later and an Israelite is going to leave the land of promise and go to Moab just to *sojourn,* to stay awhile, in a place that does not acknowledge the one true God. In fact, they worship a false god with child sacrifice. It seems like a questionable proposition.

This man was leaving Bethlehem-judah, the name by definition being the house of bread and praise. Granted there was a famine but was the Lord unable? Had this man forgotten how the Lord fed the children of Israel in the wilderness when they ran out of supply from Egypt? Or did he worry that although God did it back then, God was no longer able or willing? Had he come to trust more in himself than in God? We will see if this decision was in his best interest. At any rate, he was going to move. This man was determined to go and *sojourn.*

In The Country

We might say countryside instead of just country. The Hebrew word sadeh can also be translated field. There was an area in Moab called the field as opposed to the mountains or shoreline. It is actually a plateau about 4,500 feet above the Dead Sea. It was (still is) extremely fertile and well watered. Prevailing westerly winds often bring clouds from over the Mediterranean and across Israel without dropping any rain until over this sadeh (field – *country of Moab.)*

OF MOAB

The country of Moab was due east of Israel on the other side of the Dead Sea. During the time of the Judges, Israel and Moab were sometimes at war with one another and sometimes at peace for as long as eighty years. One of the greatest men in all of Biblical history is buried in the land that was Moab. God himself buried Moses on Mount Nebo overlooking the Promised Land.

The progenitor of the Moabites was a man named Moab. He was the son of Lot. Lot was the son of Abraham's brother Haran who died before Abraham left Ur. When God called Abraham to leave Ur, his father and nephew went with him. Abraham's father died and still, everywhere Abraham went, Lot went too.

They went to Canaan and later to Egypt and then back to Canaan. Abraham looked out for his nephew and rescued him from desperate situations. They were to eventually separate when the area they were in did not have enough pasture to sustain both men's flocks of sheep and other livestock. Abraham let Lot choose which ground he wanted and Lot chose the best for himself. It was near the sin cities of Sodom and Gomorrah. Abraham moved on.

After some time, Lot and his family moved into the wicked city of Sodom and he became an important figure in government. Eventually God destroyed these cities and ultimately only Lot and his two daughters escaped judgment.

Perhaps because of the wicked influence of the city they had called home, these daughters later decided to get their father drunk and have children by him to preserve their father's line. These incestuous relationships produced two sons. They named them Moab and Ben-ammi; thus began the Moabite and the Ammonite nations.

God gave both nations a land but at some point in time these two nations no longer worshipped the one true God. Maybe it went as far back as their father Lot. Did Lot become discouraged because of the way in which his two sons were conceived? Did he give up and not tell them about how much he had been blessed by the Lord? God told Abraham He would bless him because He knew Abraham would teach his children after him. Perhaps Lot did not teach them. Or was it the influence of their mothers? We do not know but we do know that somewhere along the line the people of Moab and Ammon began idol worship.

Years later when their relatives, the children of Israel, came out of Egypt and were heading to the Promised Land, God told Israel not to fight with the children of Moab or Ammon because He had given them their land. However, God did have certain strict stipulations concerning the children of Moab and Ammon:

> "An Ammonite or Moabite shall not enter into the congregation of the LORD; even to their tenth generation shall they not enter into the congregation of the LORD forever: because they met you not with bread and with water in the way, when ye came forth out of Egypt; and because they hired against

> thee Balaam the son of Beor of Pethor Mesopotamia, to curse thee. Nevertheless the LORD thy God would not hearken unto Balaam; but the LORD thy God turned the curse into a blessing unto thee, because the LORD thy God loved thee." Deuteronomy 23:3-5

The Moabites were not allowed to enter into the congregational worship with Israel throughout their generations because of the way they had treated their cousins, the children of Israel, when they were journeying on their way to the Promised Land.

The children of Israel wanted to pass through Moab and promised not to bother the Moabites but instead to stay strictly to the highway. (The Kings Highway ran between Damascus, the oldest continuously inhabited city in the world, situated to the far north, all the way south down to Egypt.)

As well as promising never to leave the highway, they also wanted to buy provisions from the Moabites. They were willing to pay for water. (Talk about nothing new under the sun!) It seems like it would have been a great business opportunity for the people of Moab. But all requests were refused and since the Lord had already told the Israelites that they were not to fight with the Moabites they turned to take the long way around.

The Moabites, just for good measure no doubt, hired Balaam, a prophet, to call down curses against the children of Israel. He was willing to exploit the gift given to him by God, for money. He agreed to curse Israel. He did his best but the only thing that came out of his mouth was blessing. God was looking out for His people and He turned curses to blessing. He still does.

Archaeologists have discovered that even centuries later

(after the time of Ruth) the Moabite language was still a dialect of Hebrew. They kept the talk but not the walk and tragically not their God.

The Moabite system of government was headed by kings. They were already a strong nation when the children of Israel reached the Promised Land. Geographically the country was about twenty-five miles wide and approximately forty–five miles long. It was between the desert and the Dead Sea. God blessed them with a good land but they did not bless the name of the Lord.

He And His Wife And His Two Sons

We learn that this man has a wife and two sons. Not only is he leaving Bethlehem, but he is also taking his family with him. He alone is responsible for the decision to leave Bethlehem, however, because it has been clearly stated that it is he that went. It is only after we are told that he went that we are again told that he went *and* that his wife and children accompany him. This is what we would expect since Biblically the man is to be the head of his house and ultimately is responsible to God for his family.

Was taking his family to Moab wise? It meant putting his family in a place where there was no Word of God. These people, the Moabites, did not worship the Lord. They did not honor Him and keep His feast days. They did not keep His commandments. They did not know Him. They did not love Him. This man was taking his family to a place of spiritual famine.

> *Ruth 1:2 "And the name of the man was Elimelech, and the name of his wife Naomi, and the name of his two*

sons, Mahlon and Chilion, Ephrathites of Bethlehem-judah. And they came into the country of Moab, and continued there."

And The Name Of The Man Was Elimelech

Giving this certain man's name in the text again shows us, how very much God is interested in the individual. He is not just looking at mankind in an over-seeing innocuously benevolent sort of way. He knows our name. Not only is the focused spotlight on an individual, but also, the individual is named. His name is Elimelech.

During Biblical times, the meaning of names was especially significant. Loving and doting parents chose names for their little ones, which expressed their hopes for that child. They prayed and encouraged those characteristics embodied in the name. As a child grew, these were the qualities parents wanted to see developed in their child.

Obadiah would be encouraged to be "a servant of God." Nathaniel would be encouraged to be a "gift of God." In naming a child, with all the love and concern that his parents had, they can then pray and guide their little one to display these characteristics. With the privilege of naming a child came the responsibility of helping the child to live up to the name that had been lovingly chosen. Eventually, the child reaches an age when the privilege of having his name and the responsibility of embodying those characteristics becomes his own.

There are many examples of men of God who did live up to their names. There are also examples of men who did not. Absolom meant "father's peace". Absolom, however, broke his father David's heart and did not give him peace. Solomon named his son Rehoboam, "an enlarger". He did not enlarge the kingdom he inherited; he lost a large part of it.

Elimelech's name means, "My God is King." When his parents named Elimelech, they were making a statement and it was a statement about their belief in God. They wanted their baby boy to have a name that proclaimed their belief. They desired that all of his life he would acknowledge that the God of Israel and the whole world is his God and King.

During the time of the Judges, Israel had no man that was king like the nations around them had. Eventually, they did want an earthly king. It must have made God sad. He said that the people were rejecting Him as King. But in this time there was at least one little boy whose name acknowledged that not only is God King but also that God is my King; *Elimelech,* what a wonderful name.

And His Wife's Name Was Naomi

As in the case of Elimelech, we have the defining role for this woman before we have her name. She is a wife. (A certain man had a wife. See preceding verse.) Since the beginning of time, God had ordained marriage (see Genesis 2). It was not good for man to live alone. Man was given a helper. Marriage gave this woman a specific role in life. Marriage gives her a defined status in the community. She had entered into a covenant relationship with her husband. She is the wife of a certain man who, we have already been told, was from Bethlehem-judah, of the tribe of Judah. Judah was one of the twelve sons of the ancient patriarch Jacob.

Just before Jacob's death, he called all of his sons to gather around him and he prophesied over them one by one. Of Judah he says:

> "The scepter shall not depart from Judah, nor a lawgiver from between his feet, until Shiloh come; and unto him shall the gathering of the people be." Genesis 49:10

There is much more to this prophetic blessing, which can be found in the verses preceding and following this one verse. What is interesting here is the promise of a king descending from Judah. This king was to be a lawgiver as well. There is also a promise that this kingly line would last forever. So far, even though in the book of Ruth, we are now generations and hundreds of years later, the prophecy about a descendent of Judah being a king had not come true. But God has a time, a perfect time, and perfect timing to work out all His promises and the people trusted, waited, and never forgot the promise.

Did this wife of Elimelech ask the Lord to work out His purposes and promises in and through her daily life? And this woman, defined by her role as a wife, is named Naomi, which means beautiful, comely, pleasant, and graceful. Surely her parents thought she possessed all those lovely attributes and they also must have taught her the importance of having an inner beauty.

And The Name Of His Two Sons, Mahlon And Chilion

It would seem that the meaning of some names have changed. Perhaps this could be caused by the characteristics of the person with the name. We have all had those negative reactions to certain names. We all say, "I would never name a child _____or _____ because I knew a person I certainly did not admire with that name." A similar change has occurred with the names of Mahlon and Chilion. The older information we have suggests these names meant "ornament" and "joy" based on the Hebrew root. Today's commentaries suggest they mean sickly and pining and whining. It seems very difficult to imagine doting parents with unabashed pride in their firstborn little baby, naming him "sickly," or later naming his younger brother "pining and whining". Parents just do not give their children such terrible names.

There is, admittedly, the case of Eli's grandson being named Ichabod, which means, "the glory of the Lord is departed." His mother, who named him, probably knew that her husband had been unfaithful to her with the women he met as a priest in the Tabernacle. Then the Philistines had come. Eli's sons lost their lives in the battle. Eli, who was a prophet and priest, dropped dead. The Ark of the Covenant where God met the children of Israel in the Tabernacle is captured and during all of this, Eli's daughter-in-law gives birth. It is no wonder she names the little baby Ichabod, "the glory has departed."

However, in the case of Elimelech and Naomi, there was no reason to give their boys such awful names as sickly and pining and whining.

The family was well off financially. Also, they were from an old and respected family and had high standing in the community. They were leading the good life with two little boys who were an ornament and a joy to their parents. The names were *Mahlon and Chilion.*

Ephrathites Of Bethlehem-judah,

As we have seen before, the town of Ephrath already existed in the days of Jacob and was later renamed Bethlehem. This did not happen for some time after the conquest of the Promised Land. We do not know the meaning of the ancient name but after the people of Israel had been settled there for some time, they noted the wonderful crops that they were able to harvest and renamed their town with a Hebrew name. They aptly named it Bethlehem, which as has been stated means house of bread.

The family of Elimelech was one of the older families that lived in Bethlehem. They were Ephrathites before Ephratha was renamed Bethlehem and the name stuck with the family. This could be the first defining indicator that this is a well-off and well-to-do family. Very often the older families of a community, who have been there the longest, have established themselves in high positions socially, politically, and financially.

And They Came Into The Country Of Moab

Elimelech had decided to make the move to Moab. The scene must have been busy with the preparations for moving to a distant place. They had no certain idea of when they would return. They would be gone at least a couple of years until the crop and pasture land situation turned around. We can see the boys running back and forth with excitement. They ask, "Can I take this with me?" "What is it like there, Dad?" "Can I go tell my friends?" "Will I have any friends there?" "Will they like me?" "What kind of house will we live in?"

Naomi must have had many questions too but probably did not ask as many as the boys may have. She stood solidly behind her husband as a wife committed to him. There were so many goodbyes. They knew everyone in the town. It was hard to say goodbye but they were going for a very good reason weren't they? A family had to eat. It was true that they had enough for now but who knew how long the famine would last? It certainly seemed to make eminent sense to try and save what they had and invest in a new life in a more propitious area didn't it? So the family made the journey and came into the countryside of Moab where they set up a new life.

And Continued There.

They *continued there.* Time passed and the family settled into the daily routines of life. We can imagine Elimelech planting crops and harvesting crops on these fertile plains. The people around them worship Chemosh but they do not get involved in that. They worship their own God and there is a live and let live attitude. The family survives. And that was what was important after all, they must have reasoned. They might have lost everything and even died of hunger if they had stayed in Bethlehem.

As far as they knew, the famine was still on in Bethlehem. How did all those left behind survive? They must be running through all their resources by now. It is a good thing we left when we did, they must have thought. They must have gone on thinking it was all in their best interests to stay because there were no plans to return to Bethlehem and they *continued there.* The verb continued could also be translated to remain.

An unspecified amount of time is elapsing. It is purposely not mentioned how much time elapsed. It is not important and further, the amount is not the point. The change in thinking was what was important. Whether the change took place over a short or long period does not alter, modify, or justify the change. Somewhere during this passage of unspecified time, the line was crossed. The steps were possibly so gradual as to be imperceptible to them. But, a line was crossed. They went from sojourning to remaining.

Perhaps there was never a conscious declaration to remain, but Moab was comfortable enough and there would always be "someday." But God, who gives us this story, knows the heart. And then there are the children. What about the children? In the meantime, the boys are growing up to become young men and although they may have heard and learned about their heritage and even participated in their religion, what were they learning by example?

> *Ruth 1:3 "And Elimelech, Naomi's husband, died, and she was left, and her two sons."*

And Elimelech

And Elimelech, the main character of the story so far, the certain man who went to sojourn, the man with a wife and two sons, the man who is an Israelite living in a foreign country, he is gone, with the story only just begun. His life has been lived and is over. We will hear of his doings no more. His final resting place is in Moab. His sojourn is over but he will not go home again.

Naomi's Husband

Subtly, subtly, oh so subtly the spotlight has shifted and the focus is now on Naomi. (The craftsmanship of this story is exquisite throughout. It is prose that is close to poetry in its ability to say so much in distillate form.) Naomi alone represents the couple that went to Moab. She is the one who will make the decisions for the family. From now on we see Elimelech only in the recollection of his relationship to Naomi. Naomi is now the central figure. The importance of Elimelech to the story lies only in the fact that he was *Naomi's husband.*

Died

Died. That is all, just one terse stark word and no more. We do not know what caused his death. We do not know the circumstances of how he died. We are given just one sparse unvarnished word. *Died.* The shock is great. It happened so quickly. We have only just begun to know this man and suddenly he is gone. We were given no warning, no reason for his death. If there was some reason, some explanation, we could understand. We could have been a little prepared. One is never really prepared for death, even when a person seems to linger near death and we somewhat anticipate it. Death is still incomprehensible. But the suddenness of this death takes us unawares. We have reached an end. And Naomi, poor Naomi, how was she to go on?

And She Was Left

Elimelech was gone *and she was left.* She had been a wife for so many years. They had shared so much, just the two of them. They were so happy with the birth of their firstborn. Our ornament they called him. The baby made their life so full, so wonderful. The fun they had with him, his first tooth and watching him take those first unsteady steps. He would fall but they were so proud of the way he got right back up. And those first baby words, no one could understand them but they could.

And then came their second son. He made their joy overflowing. He made their joy complete. They would always acknowledge this. They called him Chilion, which means joy. He was more bold perhaps than his older brother had been. They were all good memories, precious memories. But, why God, why? Could it be explained? Could it ever be understood?

And Her Two Sons

We know the names of the boys but the names are not mentioned here. They are seen cast together as a unit. Because the focus is on Naomi, they are seen as *her two sons.* The sons have importance here not as individuals but in terms of who they are in relationship to Naomi, *her sons.*

Until this point they were always referred to as his sons and ultimately his responsibility in every aspect of life. While it was true that they were supposed to listen to Naomi and honor and respect her, Elimelech as their father held ultimate authority and responsibility. Now they are her sons.

Their importance, at this point in this story, and here in this verse, is because of the fact that they are of the unit, the family; the ones who are left. What does that mean? Left? Left to do what?

Most strikingly it means that life has changed. They no longer have a father to look to as head of the family. They no longer have a father to look to for advice or comfort in difficult situations. Most of all, they no longer have a father to look to as spiritual leader. And, they are in a spiritually difficult place; surrounded by people who are involved in a wicked religion that demands wicked practices (such as temple prostitution and child sacrifice which involved throwing babies into the flames of Chemosh.)

In a real way, they have lost a shield, a buffer, between who they are as part of God's people, and the Moabite world around them. Although Naomi still represents the unit of two that became one, that is, their parents, they are not accustomed to looking to her as head of the household. They cannot see in her, the spiritual authority that was over them. There is an irreplaceable father gone from their lives. There is a void, which cannot be filled.

They are now more responsible than ever for their relationship to God. They cannot lean on the faith of their father. Their faith must now stand on its own. Israel and all that Israel represents in the way of worship, prayer, and the celebrations of holidays, has just moved farther away.

> *Ruth 1:4 "And they took themselves wives of the women of Moab; the name of the one was Orpah, and the name of the other, Ruth, and they dwelt there about ten years."*

And They Took

The Hebrew word for took is nasa and the primary meaning is to lift or raise up. It also means to elevate or extol or exalt. Examples of nasa would include:

> "Save thy people, and bless thine inheritance: feed them also, and lift them up (nasa) forever." Psalms 28:9

> "I will lift up (nasa) mine eyes unto the hills, from whence cometh my help." Psalms 121:1

Psalms 120 to 134 were the songs that the pilgrims sang when they went up to Jerusalem to have their sin forgiven and to worship the Lord. They had to literally go up because Jerusalem is some 5000 feet above sea level.

The word nasa also means "to bear" as to bear sin. Way back in the beginning of time, after Cain slew Abel, God punished him. He told him that the ground that he tilled would no longer yield to him and that he would be a fugitive and a vagabond.

> "And Cain said unto the Lord, My punishment is greater than I can bear (nasa.)" Genesis 4:13

Another use of nasa is illustrated when just before the children of Israel were to enter the Promised Land, they sent in twelve spies to spy out the land for forty days. Two came back with a glowing report but the other ten did not. Their reports were very negative. They said the land could never be conquered. They spread fear among the people. The people wailed and lamented. They cried and they regretted ever leaving Egypt. It would be better to still be slaves. Because of their unbelief, God was angry and punished them saying:

> "After the number of the days in which ye searched the land, even forty days, each day for a year, shalt ye bear (nasa) your iniquities, even forty years, and ye shall know my breach of promise." Numbers 14:34

And not one of these people, over the age of twenty, lived to go into the Promised Land except the two faithful spies. They all did bear (nasa) their punishment.

But being a loving God, God did provide a way so that the people would not have to bear (nasa) other sins. They could come to the Tabernacle, and later, when it was built, to the Temple. There they could offer sacrifices. The priest would make sacrifices of atonement for the sin of the entire congregation. He also brought in two live goats. One was sacrificed and with the other he placed both hands on the goat's head and confessed all the iniquities of the people.

> "And the goat shall bear (nasa) upon him all their iniquities unto a land not inhabited: and

> he shall let go the goat in the wilderness."
> Leviticus. 16:22

The second goat figuratively took (nasa) away the sins of the people.

The word nasa also means forgiven. In the death of innocent life the sin was both borne away and forgiven.

> "Blessed is he whose transgression is forgiven (nasa), whose sin is covered."
> Psalms 32:1

> "I acknowledge my sin unto thee, and mine iniquity have I not hid. I said, I will confess my transgressions unto the LORD; and thou forgavest (nasa) the iniquity of my sin."
> Psalms 32:5

Lifted up (nasa) is closely used with salvation from the deadliness of sin. We see this in the life of Noah when God saved him and his family from amidst a wicked and doomed world of sin.

> "And the flood was forty days upon the earth, and waters increased; and bare up (nasa) the ark and it was lifted up (nasa) above the earth. Genesis 7:17

How does the taking of wives equate with these definitions of nasa? Why would marriage be the lifting up or bearing up of a woman? What immediately comes to mind is a young husband lifting up his bride to carry her over the threshold. But the meaning of that has been lost and what remains is the tradition.

We can go back to the very first marriage for insight.

God gave Eve to Adam. He took his wife from the hand of God. It then became his responsibility to support her, to defend her, to lift her up in prayer and praise. He was to lift her up to a place of safety and security, physically, emotionally and spiritually. What an awesome responsibility! We see in nasa, a part of God's perfect plan for marriage. For the wives of Mahlon and Chilion it is now a possibility to have this nasa in their lives; for them to be lifted up in a marriage that honors God.

Themselves Wives

Between the last word of the last verse (sons) and the first words of this verse there are no mentioned events in the lives of our characters. With extreme abruptness we go from sons who have lost a father to sons who have married, leading us to wonder about the haste. One action is definitely combined with the other (the death of Elimelech and the marriage of the two sons.) We see them left, and they took *themselves wives*. The two pieces of information are linked together with a single word of union, ***and.***

What was it in their character that would lead to such unseemly haste? They did not get their mother to arrange the whole thing as was common during this time period. We even have an account of one of the judges of Israel (Samson) asking his parents to get him a bride (and she was not a girl from Israel either). It is clear that this is something they did on their own; *they took.*

And again, this is almost immediately after the death of their father. They may have been rebounding from the death of their father and hoped to find comfort. On the other hand, it may have been their father's death that freed them from his disapproval of the idea of them taking *wives of the women of Moab.* But Elimelech had died and there was no stopping them now. There were no longer the constraints of religion or tradition. *They took themselves wives.*

Of The Women Of Moab;

The women of Moab were renowned for their beauty. They had been particularly attractive to the men of Israel. When they were heading for the Promised Land, they came to the border of Moab. Many of the men started having affairs with the women of Moab. Enticed by these women, they entered into eating food sacrificed to idols and bowing down to their false god. God was angry and many men died (24,000) because of what they had done. God had already told the children of Israel that they were to only marry other Israelites and not women from foreign nations because He knew the Israelites would eventually be enticed to worship other gods. The commandment was clear.

> "Neither shalt thou make marriages with them; thy daughter thou shalt not give unto his son, nor his daughter shalt thou take unto thy son. For they will turn away thy son from following me, that they may serve other gods: so will the anger of the Lord be kindled against you, and destroy thee suddenly." Deuteronomy 7:3 and 4

We now see the danger of moving to and staying on in a place of sin. There is the temptation to marry outside the people of God. What was the judgment for this disobedience? Sudden death.

The Name Of The One Was Orpah And The Name Of The Other Ruth

Orpah became the bride of Chilion. Since the name of Orpah is given first we may assume that this marriage took place first. This is a little unusual since Chilion was the younger son. It could be an indicator of character traits. Often, the first-born in a family is the more serious and responsible and the younger child is more carefree and happy-go-lucky. If this were true in this family, we can understand why it would be easier for the second son to break with tradition and his religious upbringing, to marry a Moabite woman.

Since the timing of the wedding is linked to the death of the father, it shows that Chilion felt all restraints loosened with the passing of his father. Either his mother did not try to stop this marriage, or, understandably overcome with grief, she did not have the strength to oppose her sons' decisions. If she did try to stop Chilion and then Mahlon, either her protests were too weak or Chilion simply ignored his mother. For all we know he could have been courting this young lady (perhaps secretly) for some time. At any rate, the decision was made and Chilion married Orpah.

Once the younger son was seen by his older brother to be happily married, it must have encouraged the older son to follow suit. The older son married a Moabite woman named Ruth.

Both sons were very happy in their marriages and their mother Naomi, the pleasant one, was happy too. We will see, that Naomi's daughters-in-law came to adopt the Israelite faith and Naomi grew to love them each very much.

The meaning of the name Orpah is fawn or deer. Perhaps she had big beautiful brown eyes. The meaning of Ruth is beautiful. Other meanings for the names of Mahlon, Chilion, Orpah and Ruth have crept into commentaries, probably starting with Jerome (342-420AD.) Jerome was a linguist and a commentator of the Bible and exceptional for his day. He translated the Bible into Latin from the Hebrew and the Greek and thus the Vulgate translation.

In giving the meaning of Biblical names however, he often used circular reasoning. Ruth was a faithful friend to Naomi and thus her name must mean faithful friend. Orpah turned back, therefore, her name must mean stiff-necked, a person too stubborn to adopt the Israelite faith. Jerome assumed this because Orpah did not return to Bethlehem with Naomi.

He reasoned that Mahlon must have gotten sick and that caused his death, so his name must have meant sickly. Since Chilion also died, he too must have been sick and because of his sickness he probably whined and pined, so his name meant whining and pining.

For Jerome's meanings of the names to be accurate would indicate an incredible prophetic insight on the part of not only an Israelite couple but also two sets of Moabite parents in a pagan country.

And They

The words *and they* represent the entire family. It has always been about the family and will continue to be about the family. The sons have married and the family now numbers five and will hopefully increase in the future. Each son is the head of his own household and each is responsible to God for his family. With his wife by his side to lend him her help, insights, and love, each son will make and bear the responsibilities of all the final decisions for his family.

Dwelt

The Hebrew word that is translated as dwelt is yashab. It literally means to sit down. In order to leave a seated position it is necessary first to stand before you can walk in any direction. It is obvious that there is no thought of going back to Israel. The family was sitting and fitting fairly comfortably into the society around them. They had close ties through marriage to other families in the community. The sons were starting families of their own in Moab. They *dwelt.*

There

Again we see the fine-tuned craftsmanship displayed in the telling of this story. The text at this point does not name Moab even though we already know that Moab is definitely the place where the family dwelt. The word used is *there* as opposed to here. We are clearly viewing them *there* in the country of Moab. It says *there* because the position from which we are viewing is, and always will be, Bethlehem. We are viewing the family from the perspective of being in the Promised Land in general and Bethlehem in particular. We stand in Bethlehem and see the family go away. They are over *there*. We are here and view them over *there*.

About Ten Years

The sons had married and Orpah and Ruth are now a part of this family. Naomi has had a chance to come to love the two young wives, not only because of what they mean to her sons, but also, as we shall see, what they mean to her. She has had time to teach the young women about the God of Israel. We have seen the family through a move to a foreign country, the loss of Elimelech, and the marriage of the two sons.

The family has lived in Moab for *about ten years.* Ten is a number connected with completeness, law, judgment, and our response or responsibility to God. It is interesting that there were ten generations from Adam to Noah. Noah was singled out for the greatest move of God upon the earth since Adam and creation. And why did God choose Noah? God choose Noah because Noah was both just and true. He found grace in the sight of the Lord. In a world that had gone completely wicked in all its ways, Noah stood, and stood out as a man of God. And then came the judgment of a wicked world. God made a covenant with Noah. God started over with a family.

There were ten generations from Noah to Abraham. God again started something new. God made a covenant with Abraham. Again He was working with a family, the family of Abraham.

Another place we see the importance of the number ten is in the giving of the law to the children of Israel, the Ten Commandments. And yet another place the number ten was important was in the tabernacle. It was ten cubits long and had ten linen curtains. We have one of our responses and responsibilities to God in the number ten with our tithes. We are to give one tenth, or ten percent, to God.

As we continue, we are told that the family has lived in Moab for *about ten years*. This reference to the ten year time period is a summary note to all that has taken place thus far. The famine, the introduction to the family, the decision to go to Moab, the death of the father, the marriages, have all happened in this ten year time period. What is going to happen next?

Ruth 1:5 "And Mahlon and Chilion died also both of them; and the woman was left of her two sons and her husband."

And Mahlon And Chilion Died

Again we have the conjunction *and.* This simple word connects the previous phrase of *dwelt there about ten years* with *Mahlon and Chilion died.* There is, again, no warning of sickness or battle injuries or murder. The bald statement of death comes to us, again suddenly, without explanation except perhaps for the little connecting word *and.*

Also

Also reminds us of the death of Elimelech. The three are connected for several reasons. The first and most obvious connection is that Mahlon and Chilion are related to Elimelech. They are Elimelech's sons. The second connection is in the act of dying. Are the deaths connected by the same cause? The description of the deaths, or rather lack of description, is exactly the same. But both the death of the father and the deaths of the sons follow directly after we are told that they continued or remained in Moab.

The third reason that they are connected is because all three constitute Naomi's entire family.

And the fourth and most profound reason these deaths are connected is because of the changes the deaths will cause in Naomi's life, thinking, and decisions. Collectively all three men were the visible foundation upon which Naomi's whole life, her whole world, rested.

Both Of Them;

Saying *both of them,* emphasizes that this is all, the total, Naomi has no more. Her bereavement takes on a universal emptiness. Nowhere is there any hope of being connected to a family. A great deal of one's identity is connectedness. We take delight in the loosest connections; as in knowing someone who knows someone who knows someone. Studies have been made to show that the whole world is connected by as small a number as six (someone knowing someone who knows someone and so forth only up to six connections and we are connected to every person in the world). It is referred to as six degrees of separation.

But this is no longer a connected Naomi. This is a woman bereft. She had lost her husband and now her two sons, *both of them.*

And The Woman

The woman, is not named here as Naomi but of course we know her identity. The focus of the story is still on Naomi and even though she is not named, we still know it is she. It is not a mistake or an oversight that her name is not mentioned. What is to be emphasized is that here is a woman, outside of her natural social setting and culture, and she is bereft of her men folk. Once again, we find the art, the poetry, brilliantly displayed. In this distillate of words, *and the woman,* there is statement, meaning, nuance, suggestion, description, delineation, and even prediction.

There are no mistakes or idle words in the Bible. Every word is put there for a divine reason. By using the word woman rather than her name, the author accomplishes several things. The tragedy of her bereavement is identified, emphasized and amplified in the simplicity of a single word as a universal experience rather than that of one individual. This woman's experience could be the experience of any woman. It could be our experience. Using the word woman, also allows the focus to be on the extreme nature of her bereavement.

She is a woman alone. She has no visible means of support, not physical, not emotional, nor spiritual. Not giving her name reinforces the fact that she has lost her identity. No more is she a wife and a mother. She is simply a woman; a helpmeet to no one, a mother to no one. Hers is a stripped bare life in the extreme of bereavement, bereft not a little, bereft three times, bereft of all.

If Naomi had been named here, we would then be looking at her and thinking of her as a personality with her own peculiar feelings and emotions rather than at her position as a woman. The Hebrew word used here for woman is ishshah. Ishshah can be used in various roles to mean a female person as in:

> "And the rib, which the LORD God had taken from man, made He woman, (ishshah) and brought her unto the man." Genesis 2:22

This verse goes all the way back to the beginning when God created woman from man and then gave her to him a separate being yet a very part of him. Ishshah means woman.

In this phrase *and the woman,* we go back to the first verse of the book of Ruth where we first meet Naomi not as an individual but as a wife an ishshah as in:

> "Therefore shall a man leave his father and his mother, and shall cleave unto his wife: (ishshah) and they shall be one flesh." Genesis 2:24

Her whole significance in that first verse of the book of Ruth is in her being married to her husband. It was more important to know what she was (a wife) than who she was (Naomi.) Ishshah means wife. Being a wife was her introduction to us. And now we have come full circle. The curtain has closed on this scene. We did not know who she was when we first saw her in sepia, but we came to know her in full color and now it is as if we fade again to sepia and see her only as *the woman*.

Ishshah can also mean widow as in:

> "If brethren dwell together, and one of them die, and have no children, the wife (ishshah) of the dead shall not marry without unto a stranger," Deuteronomy 25:5a.

Here in the fifth verse of the book of Ruth we see simply *the woman*. She is seen without further definition of her life. She remains the same original person, *the woman*. Seemingly that is all she has left of her identity. Her added trappings as wife and mother no longer exist.

Was Left Of Her Two Sons And Her Husband

This one lone woman *was left*. To have her whole world buried beneath an alien landscape would cause anyone to feel hopelessness and despair. Her two sons were dead and she had already lost her husband. She alone was left.

The future held out nothing to her except loneliness and aloneness. What was left to her? Her whole meaning in life had vanished into a world without meaning and a foreign world at that.

The story could end here. There are many other characters in the Bible of whom we know even less. This woman has every reason to give up on life. She alone *was left of her two sons and her husband.*

There is a point where grief becomes morbid and causes the decay of all around it. This is a state of sinful morbidity. It denies the living and it denies duty to the living. It denies one's purpose for living. Naomi was not guilty of this sin. She displays true strength of character.

Part two –
The Trip Back to Bethlehem and Ruth's Profound Vow
Ruth 1:6 to Ruth 1:18

Ruth 1:6 "Then she arose with her daughters-in-law, that she might return from the country of Moab: for she had heard in the country of Moab how that the LORD had visited his people in giving them bread."

Then She Arose

These three words have to be amongst the most exciting in the entire book of Ruth. These three words are charged with purpose and energy. These three words changed the course of history and the direction of the lives of all the characters in this book. And all Naomi did was to get up.

It was she and she alone who arose. The pronoun is singular and this is important. Naomi had hit a very low point. It would have been so very easy to give up and lie down and die, first spiritually and then physically. She could then have been buried next to her husband and forgotten forever.

But hitting bottom did not become the place to bury her. Hitting bottom worked for her benefit. It gave her a place to stand and stand she did. Naomi is incredible and her profound secret is that her incredibility comes very simply from being true to who she is. Naomi is a very practical and decisive woman. She sorrows deeply. She has lost much and there is little to live for. But she picks herself up and is decisive. She arises. The Hebrew word is qum and means to rise up. The first time it is used in the Bible, God is talking to Abraham and saying:

> "Arise, (qum) walk through the land in the length of it and in the breath of it; for I will give it unto thee." Genesis 13:17

All that was requested of Abraham was to get out of his seated position and to arise and walk. And here we see Naomi about to do the same thing. *Then she arose.* She has no doubt decided, after a survey of her options, that she will return just as they had purposed to do in the beginning. Perhaps, in the daily life in Moab, they had lost sight of those earlier intentions. Even though almost all of the family had been lost to this world before the long hoped for day of return, now Naomi decides the time has come.

Death is attended by the living with the memories of times gone by. It would have been only natural for Naomi to contemplate, with nostalgia, the fond memories of long ago in Israel; her wedding, the birth of her precious babies, the times with family and friends. The memories were so far away, not only in time, far away in distance too. Those memories were all in Bethlehem where there was still the home they had lived in and the fields that Elimelech had planted. So, *she arose.*

With Her Daughters-In-Law

Naomi continues to feel responsible for her daughters-in-law as head of this bereaved family. She is taking charge of their lives. She is making decisions for the three of them. The first thing she does is to arise. She is no longer going to sit there paralyzed by grief, wondering what is going to happen to her next. She does not picture herself sitting there for the rest of her life dwelling in the past and bewailing what might have been. She does not sit there dissolving in tears until her whole life just melts away. She arises, takes a stand on a decision with purpose in her eyes. And she is the one we see in charge. Her daughters-in-law are swept along with Naomi's new plans for their future.

That She

This pronoun *she* refers to Naomi. It is important to make note of this singular pronoun again. There can be no mistaking the fact that Naomi alone is the person who will take action. It is her decision to act. The responsibility for the action is hers alone.

Might Return From The Country Of Moab

One feels that bells and whistles ought to go off at this point or at the very least there ought to be three exclamation points!!! With center stage still in Bethlehem we are going to see the remnant of this family return. They are coming home. Once the decision had been made the anticipation for that actual moment of leaving must have been great.

The women had to make preparations, what to take and what to give away. The young women were excited to be going "home" but what was home like? Naomi would have told them before about life in Israel but this time they listened more carefully. There must have been a stream of questions without end. This was where they were going to live for the rest of their lives. Would they like life in Bethlehem? Yes, Naomi reassured them. Just wait. She would show them everything; the places where Mahlon and Chilion loved to play, the house where they used to live. They would love it. Elimelech had always meant for them to go home someday. He did not live to see the day but now they were actually going home. Things would be different though. Would her old friends remember her, Naomi may have wondered with silent questions of her own.

For She Had Heard In The Country Of Moab

There might not have been newspapers, the TV evening news, or telecommunications but word did travel throughout the countryside. It would not have been extraordinary for reports circulating about Israel to have come to the attention of Naomi. Everyone knew she was an Israelite and news from there would have naturally been shared with her. And so she heard. There are perhaps what we could call outer hearing and inner hearing. There is a hearing of information with the physical ear and there is a hearing of the spirit and soul. The LORD taught this when He gave the great Shema:

> "Hear, (shema) O Israel: The LORD our God
> is one LORD: And thou shalt love the LORD

> thy God with all thine heart, and with all thy soul, and with all thy might. And these words, which I command thee this day, shall be in thine heart:" Deuteronomy 6:4-6

These words were to be said over and over and are still said by observing Jews today, the world over, both morning and night. And they were to be taught to their children diligently. Yes, God used the word diligently. The actual Hebrew word is shanan, which literally means to sharpen as a sword, to pierce through, to inculcate, to enforce, and to teach.

> "And thou shalt teach them diligently (shanan) unto thy children, And shalt talk of them when thou sittest in thine house, and when thou walkest by the way, and when thou liest down, and when thou risest up." Deuteronomy 6: 7

Surely this had been taught to Naomi at an early age and she and her husband had also taught their sons this idea of critical hearing and then critical thinking which grew out of loving God. Naomi used these skills. She did more than just hear with her ears. She loved and trusted God. She heard with her spirit and soul as well as her ears.

How That The Lord Had Visited His People

Even the pagans acknowledged that God had visited His people. It was the hand of the Lord working on behalf of His people. God had taken action on behalf of His people. The Hebrew word for visit is paqad and has a broad meaning. It is an important verb in that it is used 285 times in the Old Testament. Some of the cited "visits" by God were to punish but more often they were to bless. It is interesting that the first record of paqad was on behalf of another woman. The Lord visited Sarah so that she could conceive and have a son. This visitation of a miracle to the elderly wife of Abraham, allowed for the beginning of the whole Israelite nation. (This can be found in Gen.21:1.)

Naomi had heard and it caused her to arise. She had heard with her heart and mind, and spirit and it caused her to respond by doing something new in her life. Her response to the moving of God in the lives of His people also included her daughters-in-law.

By Giving Them Bread

The famine was over. What good news this was. The reason for Elimelech's leaving Bethlehem with his family no longer existed. There must have been rejoicing and thankfulness in the Promised Land. Naomi's mind must have raced back to Bethlehem. There was bread once again in the house of bread. And because word had come from that now far away place, Naomi had a decision to make. It was no small decision.

Just at the moment when all of her life seemed in inky blackness, the word comes. Would Naomi respond by feeling all was futility? Would the irony of the news at this point seem nothing but even greater cruelty? There was blessing in Israel and Naomi was not in the place of blessing. Did this only serve to underscore the hopelessness of her situation? Did this good news cause Naomi to doubt in her God? God had given His people bread, the sustenance they needed to live. What did this mean for Naomi as far as her life was concerned?

Ruth 1:7 "Wherefore she went forth out of the place where she was, and her two daughters-in-law with her, and they went on the way to return unto the land of Judah."

Wherefore

Here then we have the reason for Naomi's arising and going forth. *Wherefore* is a word of reasoning that connects the arising with going. Naomi has made her decision based on what the Lord has done. She heard that the Lord has provided. She decides to set out, taking her daughters-in-law with her, because of the Lord's visiting Israel with bread. Naomi is a very practical woman and the Lord spoke to her through her practical nature and need. She reasoned within herself that because the Lord has visited His people in giving them bread, I will go forth. *Wherefore she went forth.*

She Went

She picks herself up (arises) and decides it is time to return. Once Naomi decided on a course of action, we can see her in a flurry of activity. Once she set out, there would be no turning back. There were some practical considerations. At this point the women are poor (Naomi states this later) and probably did not have to worry too much about material considerations of what to keep and what to give away.

Naomi had always been a pleasant friendly woman and there were probably some good-byes that were sad but her neighbors knew she would be happy going "home." So, the women pack up their few things to set forth towards new beginnings. She *went* away from Moab and all that had happened there. Yes, she *went.*

Forth

Naomi has decided to make a forward movement towards her future rather than waiting for it to come to her. Her future will be vastly different than the one written for her in Moab. Her decision to go *forth* has changed all that. She has decided to step out in faith. She has faith in the goodness that the Lord has already demonstrated in Israel.

With the Lord there is always the choice, to stay with the dead or to move to the land of blessing. Naomi has set *forth* on a journey. Does she know what will meet her at the end of the journey? No, she does not. But she does know where she is going and who will be there to meet her. So, *she went forth.*

Out Of The Place Where She Was

Naomi was moving away from a physical locality; she was also moving spiritually. Not only was she going home, to Bethlehem, she was moving back to living in the presence of the living God and trusting in Him as perhaps she never had before. She had been in a spiritually dead place. There was no Tabernacle in Moab. There was no place to offer tithes and offerings. There was no place to offer sacrifice for sins. There was no forgiveness for sin in the land of Moab.

It would have been only natural for Naomi to contemplate, with joy, the fond memories of long ago in Israel. Naomi knew there was no future, no hope in the place where she was. She had come to an end, a dead end. She needed the Lord more than perhaps she ever had before. She had to make a move, *out of the place where she was.*

And Her Two Daughters-In-Law With Her;

Not only did the young women arise with Naomi, they were in full accord with her decision to have done with the despair and immobility of remorse. They are young. It would be unnatural for them to give up on life. They have been devoted wives but they are still very much alive and cherish the inexplicable, perhaps youthfully optimistic, hope for a brighter future.

Naomi also has come to the other side of grief and holds fast to this same hope. The young women are inspired by her and feel drawn to the one person who also dearly loved them as she loved their husbands. Naomi could enter into their grief as no other. She understood what they had lost. She also perfectly understands that their lives must go on and they trust her. Because they trust her love for them, they also trust their future to her.

Naomi recognizes her responsibility to them, perhaps partially out of loyalty and love of her sons but also out of her love towards them. And so it is no difficult choice. In fact, it is not a matter of choice. These two young women are now an inseparable part of her life. She will go back to Bethlehem *and her two daughters-in-law with her.*

And They Went On The Way

Once Naomi made the decision to move her family back to Israel, the decision did not automatically put her there. The three literally had to travel on the *way*. The Hebrew word used here is derek and means trodden path. For at least part of the trip they probably used the Kings Highway, which, as was mentioned before, was a much used trade road between Damascus and Egypt. They went on a well-worn road to "home." They were not only on the way; they were on their way. There are hundreds of times that this word derek is used in the Bible. It has great spiritual significance.

Perhaps Naomi shared many of the things she had been taught as a child with her daughters-in-law as they went along on their long way. Perhaps some of the many things going through her mind were scriptures like:

> "Therefore thou shalt keep the commandments of the LORD thy God, to walk in his ways (derek), and to fear him. For the LORD thy God bringeth thee into a good land, a land of brooks of water, of fountains and depths that spring out of valleys and hills; A land of wheat and barley, and vines, and fig trees, and pomegranates; a land of oil olive, and honey; A land wherein thou shalt eat bread without scarceness, thou shalt not lack any thing in it; a land whose stones are iron, and out of whose hills thou mayest dig brass. When thou hast eaten and art full, then thou shalt bless the LORD thy God for the good land which he hath given thee." Deuteronomy 8:6-10

Thinking of the promises that the Lord had given would have been a comfort and a hope. To walk in His way, a clearly delineated highway, would lead them to the realm of blessing. He had gone before them, always, to show the way. It would be only natural for Naomi to share all this with her daughters-in-law. And the more she shared the more her own faith grew. It is a basic principle, that in giving, we get. Sharing our faith inevitably builds our faith. The journey was long and undoubtedly there were many questions. As *they went on the way,* many memories came back to Naomi and she thought much about Bethlehem-judah.

To Return

In the minds of the young women, leaving Moab was to leave their whole reality. They were leaving a real (even if unhappily bleak) future in Moab. What, must have seemed unreal, was Bethlehem and their unknown future. Moab was a real place, the only place they had ever known. Their view of Bethlehem was purely imaginary.

How could they be thinking of themselves as returning? It would have been quite natural to think of Moab as their center in life; it was. And if they had pictured themselves, now on the way, they would probably have seen themselves in their mind's eye as the people of Moab viewed them leaving. It is not, however, how we see them from a vantage point in Bethlehem.

Somewhere along the way there is a subtle change in the thinking of these women who were coming from Moab. At some point on the road, they were no longer leaving, they were returning. All of them, even the young women who had never been to Bethlehem were returning. This is only possible because the young women were truly married in the fullest and holiest sense of the word. They were so very one with their husbands that they completely identified with them and their nationality. As a consequence of this true unity, they were the family of Elimelech that was returning. They all realized and recognized that Moab had been a place of sojourn. With such subtlety, the journey along the path becomes not a leaving but a returning.

Our focus has always been from the position of Bethlehem. We saw the family leave and now ten years later, we see the family, having turned around, returning. We are no longer looking at their backs, as when they left ten years before, we are looking into their faces. How good it is to see the face of someone who has been away for a very long time, to welcome those who come home again.

Unto The Land Of Judah.

The three women had crossed a line of demarcation. Judah was where they were headed. Judeans were who they were or very shortly would be. It was just one step from one life into another. It was just one last step, to leave behind all that was their life before, into a new life.

In some ways they assumed that they had already taken that step with the first step away from what had been home. Having decided to take the first step was to have mentally taken the last. The young women already felt they were Judeans (by their marriage to Judeans) but did they know what it really meant to be a Judean? The only one who really knew among the three was Naomi.

Had Naomi given much thought to how her daughters-in law would feel about and fit into Judean society or was she just caught up with putting the old life and its grief behind her and looking forward with excitement to going home with her daughters?

> *Ruth 1:8 "And Naomi said unto her two daughters-in-law, Go, return each to her mother's house: the LORD deal kindly with you, as ye have dealt with the dead, and with me."*

And Naomi Said Unto Her Two Daughters-In-Law,

Naomi has been talking to her daughters-in-law all along the way and suddenly a realization comes to her. It has been easy to love these lovely girls. She may have had a few qualms in the beginning but they were soon put aside. It was only natural that her boys had wanted to marry and who else was there to marry in Moab except Moabite girls? It had all worked out anyway because they were all so happy. It did not really matter in the long run she had thought, as long as they were happy.

The girls had adapted to the family's religion. There was no problem there. And there was never a question about the girls returning with her. They were her daughters, they had become one with her sons and now they were her responsibility. It did not take any great mental strain. In fact, it had not taken any thought at all. But all this reminiscing and explaining about life in Israel had caused Naomi to reflect. What would these lovely young women face in Bethlehem?

Somewhere along the way, Naomi was drawn up short and faced facts. These girls of hers were Moabites. That had been all right in Moab, in fact, it was a good thing but how would it be in Judah to be a Moabite? Suddenly it must have come to her. What have I been thinking? These girls may be the dearest ones in the world to me but they are Moabites. How would they be received in Bethlehem? What kind of life do they have before them? How can they hope to be happy if I am the only one who accepts them and perhaps will be the only one who will even talk to them? It will be a horrible lonely life. I love these girls too much to want this kind of a future for them. They deserve more. I cannot be selfish and keep them near me. If I really love them, I must think of what is best for them. I must tell them what they must do.

Go, Return

Naomi decides without hesitation or even a second thought. We can see her stopping abruptly in the middle of the road, swinging round (she is in the lead) and with outstretched arm pointing in the direction from which they had come. With steadfast will and determination she says

Go, return.

It must have shocked the young women. What is she saying? After all their happy excitement and expectations what can she mean? She wants them to return where? Their husbands and homes are gone. Return to what? They had come all this way. In their minds and hearts they were going home with Naomi, not just going to her home but to their home too. What can Naomi be thinking?

Each

The actual Hebrew word that Naomi uses is ishshah (woman, a female person.) Naomi does not call them by name. We have seen the use of this word in the verses (1 and 2) where it refers to Naomi (as wife) before we actually learn her name and again (as a widow, verse 5) when we see her having lost all the men in her family. In both previous instances it was her role that was being looked at rather than her identification as the person Naomi.

In calling Ruth and Orpah ishshah, Naomi is indicating the new roles they will assume. They will no longer be seen as widows of Mahlon and Chilion, but as young unmarried women. We also see here that there are two separate homes to which they would be going. The relationship they have as being related through ties of marriage will stand no longer.

To Her Mother's House:

Return *each to her mother's house* means that the young women would be living in separate households without those bonds that have come to mean so much to each of them. They will no longer be living as sisters-in-law. It means a return to their life before marriage. Was it possible?

Can a person return to their previous life; the life they lived before? Can one take up where one left off? Could they negate all that had happened as if it had never happened? That was what going back would mean.

Perhaps there was an inducement to going back in that it would mean, to a certain extent, a carefree existence in her mother's house. There would no longer be the responsibility of wife turned widow. Each would again be cast in the role of a dependent daughter in a household run by her mother.

They had learned what it meant to be joined to a man and to have a home of their own. How could they return to being a "girl" in her mother's house? How could they go back and ignore all that being married meant?

Even more bewildering, was Naomi really asking them to turn around and walk out of her life? There would never be another chance to see her or to hear the voice of this mother-in-law who had become a mother-in-love. Turning back meant leaving her forever.

Dear, dear, practical Naomi; was being practical being wise?

The Lord Deal Kindly

Naomi could not let her beloved daughters-in-law go without a blessing. Her prayer for them was that the Lord would work in their lives with all kindness. An act of kindness takes overt action and effort. Naomi wanted these acts of kindness from the Lord on behalf of Ruth and Orpah to continue for their entire lives. Naomi is not willing to leave them to an unknown fate. She was asking for ongoing kindnesses. She was not ready to wave good-bye with a wish of, "hope everything works out for you." She wanted much more for them and she had a definite request and no small request at that.

Kindness is an act of free will. It may or may not be deserved. While the aphorism that one kind act deserves another may be valid, it is still true that each act of kindness is by free choice. Acting kindly means keeping the needs, desires, hopes, aspirations, happiness, peace, security and well being of the recipient in mind.

To be truly an act of kindness the recipient must be known and understood, to at least some extent, otherwise, though an act may be generous and benevolent, it is not necessarily kind. Kindness must be built on the foundation of relationship. Kindness builds up that relationship. Kindness comes from the heart and touches the heart. No one is kinder or knows the heart better than God.

It is obvious that the young women not only know of the God of Israel but have come to trust in Him also. Otherwise, Naomi's words would be at best empty expressions of seeming beneficence. If the daughters-in-law did not believe in God, then this prayer of Naomi's would mean nothing more to them than a conventional "good luck" wish. Naomi's prayer is much more than just a conventional expression. It is not a "good-bye and God bless you." It is not as mindless and meaningless as the "God bless you" that is said after someone sneezes.

She is looking at the life and future set before Ruth and Orpah. From the depths of her heart, is the strong and everlasting desire that God will watch over them and tenderly care for them. She is placing them in His hands and prays that throughout their lives He will in all situations show kindness to them as only He can.

Her parting desire is fully focused on them. There is total selflessness in her desires for them. In invoking God's kindness towards these young women, Naomi has given them the kindest gift of all.

With You

Naomi's desire was equally strong for each individual daughter-in-law. She desired that the Lord's hand would remain upon each life. She wanted the blessing of the Lord for both. She wanted the eye of the Lord to continually be upon them. She wanted every situation to work out for the best and especially since she knew her watch and care would no longer be possible.

She realized that she and the young women would no longer have a share in each other's lives nor would she or they be able to help and support each other with daily encouragement as had been possible before. But she knew God would always see them even though she could not. From the depths of her heart, her ardent plea was, that in the circumstances of each life she wanted for God to deal kindly with them.

As You Have Dealt With The Dead And With Me

Naomi is acknowledging that both of her daughters-in-law have always been very kind. The Hebrew word for dealt (to deal) is asah. It is an important word and has several meanings. Some of the meanings for asah include: to toil, to build, create, or construct, to fabricate or make, to offer, and to sacrifice. When Naomi says that her daughters-in-law have dealt kindly she did not mean that they had just a sweet attitude towards her and her sons. As has been said, to deal kindly takes effort. It could come close to costing one's entire life as in the story of Rahab.

Years earlier, when the children of Israel were getting ready for the conquest of Jericho, Joshua sent two spies into the city. They found themselves in a tight situation. Somehow the authorities had learned of the two spies and were looking for them. A woman named Rahab, who was a harlot, hid them. She lived on the wall of the city. In those days, walls around cities were sometimes thick enough to allow for several chariots to drive abreast on them. (Living on the wall may have been sort of like having an expensive penthouse apartment with a great view.) Rahab told these two spies that the whole city was frightened because they had heard about the Lord drying up the water of the Red Sea and about the battles that had already been won. Then, interestingly, she made a confession of faith. She said:

> "for the LORD your God, He is God in heaven above, and in earth beneath." Joshua 2:11b

Rahab saved the lives of the spies by hiding them under flax she was drying on the roof and then letting them down the outside wall of Jericho by means of a scarlet cord hanging from a window of her house. When the day of battle came, this same scarlet cord that had saved the lives of the men would also save the lives of Rahab and her immediate family as well as her kindred. She was to again hang out the scarlet cord. As the angel of death had passed over all the houses of the children of Israel that night just before the exodus from Egypt, if they displayed the scarlet blood of a slain lamb, so too would this scarlet display of the cord cause death to pass over. The lives of Rahab and her family would be spared. And so, Rahab took initiative to save not only herself but also the lives of her family. She had said to the spies:

> "Now therefore, I pray you, swear unto me by the LORD, since I have showed (asah) you kindness, that ye will also show kindness unto my father's house, and give me a true token: and that ye will save alive my

> father, and my mother, and my brethren, and my sisters, and all that they have, and deliver our lives from death. And the men answered her, Our life for yours, if ye utter not this our business. And it shall be, when the LORD hath given us the land, that we will deal (asah) kindly and truly with thee." Joshua 2:12-14

It cost Rahab to hide these spies. It could have cost her life and probably the lives of her whole family. This kindness she showed in dealing with the spies was no mere well wishing. She took an incredible risk. Because she put her faith in the LORD God, He rewarded her with far more than saving her mortal life and the lives of her family. This kind of risk taking, all out commitment to an unknown ending, was not the end of her story. She and her family were saved on the day of conquest. Beyond that, Rahab's actions were to have consequences for generations to come, as we shall see. Rahab will be remembered by all generations to come, of those who love God.

Dealing (asah) kindly then, on the part of the young women towards their husbands and Naomi, meant so much more than just a pleasant attitude. It meant to work, to create, and to build a loving relationship with not only their husbands but also with the mother of their husbands.

Naomi is gratefully stating that these young women have been all that wives can be to both her sons and to her. She acknowledges that these young women were kindness itself. She harbors no regrets for what her sons might have had, should they have married someone else. There is no bitterness towards them for any reason, large or small, whatsoever. She thinks nothing but good of them. She expresses nothing but goodness towards them. She goes further, she invokes the blessing of God upon them.

Ruth 1:9 "The Lord grant you that ye may find rest, each of you in the house of her husband. Then she kissed them; and they lifted up their voice, and wept."

The Lord Grant You

Naomi is again invoking the Lord. She is talking to her daughters-in-law as one believer to another. Naomi does not believe in a God who takes an interest in mankind only in a nominal and general way. She knows that God takes an intensely personal interest in the lives of each individual. She talks openly to Orpah and Ruth of her prayer for them with the sure confidence that they understand and can also trust God with their lives. She is not explaining anything here nor is she talking in terms that express that she fears they will not understand. Naomi proceeds in a straightforward manner because she knows that her daughters-in-law understand exactly what she is saying.

This time, she is going to be more specific. Her previous request, to the Lord, was more general and sweeping and wide. She wanted the Lord to deal in all situations of their lives in a kindly way, as perhaps a doting father would do.

Just how and when and where this kindness would occur she leaves up to God's judgment. And now she has some specific requests of God for these daughters-in-law that she loves and appreciates so much.

That Ye May Find Rest,

Naomi's request of the Lord is that these young women may find rest. She acknowledges that this rest is a gift from the Lord. True *rest* comes only from the hand of God. It is a security from want and striving and worry. It encompasses more than physical or financial security. It includes mental and emotional peace. And most of all it must also include the spiritual peace and security that can only come from God. This is the gift she is asking of God.

The Hebrew word for rest is menuchah. This *rest* is part of the promise to the children of Israel of what will be theirs in the Promised Land. This is what He will give His people.

> "For ye are not as yet come to the rest (menuchah) and to the inheritance, which the LORD your God giveth you." Deuteronomy 12:9

Two things are promised here, *rest* and an inheritance. This *rest* then is not the inheritance of the land itself that God has promised to them. The land will undoubtedly give them financial security if worked and financial security would give them a certain measure of relief from worry. The *rest* that is mentioned here is more extensive. It is the calm assurance of God being in control and watching out for His people. This is sublime security. It holds the peace that comes from His people putting their trust in Him. Naomi wants this same *rest* for her daughters-in-law, each in the house of her own husband. If there be any irony here it is in the fact that this *rest* was to be found in the Promised Land and here we see Naomi urging a return to Moab instead of heading on forward to Judah.

Each Of You

For a second time, Naomi is making clear that she is talking not in a collective bonhomie sense but to two individuals.

This is the desire of Naomi's heart for *each.* This is not a general wish for all mankind. "Good-bye, have a good life." Naomi has come to love these, her daughters-in-law, for each young woman's singularly own distinctive self. That Orpah has a secure and good life is of primary concern to her. That Ruth has a secure and good life is of utmost importance to her. She loves them *each.*

In The House Of Her Husband.

Naomi, by no means, desires her daughters-in-law, to be sacrificed on the altar of widowhood. She desires all good for them and wishes to see them remarried and established and a happy wife with (the Lord grant it) children.

The phrase, *the house of her husband* indicates the recognition of the husband being the head of the house. This was not a unisex world. Tasks were not shared equally. Each person had a purpose and role in life ordained by God. By definition a woman was to be a helper to her husband. This did not mean that her role in life was inferior in any way. She alone was responsible to God for her actions and decisions. She could even have her own business if she desired. But her intent and desire was always supposed to be that she would be a blessing to her husband. (The godly woman was later described in Proverbs 31, but that is getting ahead of our story.)

House of her husband also means family of her husband. This was a patriarchal society. In most cases we still see this today reflected in our own culture in the wife taking the name of her husband and the children having the name of their father. The wife and the children are the house of the husband and father. It gave them not only identity, it also gave them inheritance both material and spiritual.

Then She Kissed Them;

Naomi dearly loves her daughters-in- law. It had not been easy to tell them that they must part. They had been through so much together and were so close. The thought of it was bitter, very bitter. She holds them close to her for one last time. Their hair, their faces, their widening eyes, she looked into those eyes filling with hurt and tears. Naomi's eyes were filling with tears too. They were both so dear to her. *Then she kissed them.*

And They Lifted Up Their Voice

It may be wondered, how the plural *they* and *their* could lift up a singular *voice.* Again, there is the nuance of fine craftsmanship. Very simply, we see these women not as a group of three individuals, although each is very different and individual. We see them as one in harmony of spirit and soul. As a choir of a hundred voices can make one beautiful sound, so too did these three make one hauntingly sad sound, which encompassed all that they meant to each other. Together as one *they lifted up their voice.*

And Wept

Here is a bottomless deep, deep grief indeed. Here we see the three women on the road to meet their destiny and the love that binds them so closely together must hold their lives together also. It is impossible to think of separating and going in three different directions. It is impossible for these young women to face the idea of never seeing the face of their beloved mother-in-law again. And although this idea is Naomi's in wanting what is best for her daughters-in-law, it is also incredibly painful for her to think of never seeing her daughters-in-law again. For Naomi to never see them again would be the unbearable grief and finality of having not a single member of her family left to her. It cannot be thought of. It must not be, it cannot be. And yet, it is this very thought that causes their grief.

And so we see them, the three women clinging to each other, as if never letting go would keep them together. They stand there on the way in the very spot that would decide for all time their still uncertain future and their destiny. Parting is more than they can bear. Together, they *wept.*

> *Ruth 1:10 "And they said unto her, Surely we will return with thee unto thy people."*

And They Said Unto Her

The young women were the first to recover enough from weeping to try and understand this new and incomprehensible situation. Naomi had already made up her mind. Her grief at the idea of parting is deeper because it has become reality for her. But it was a complete surprise and shock to the young women. What could this mean? They questioned Naomi. It was not something that immediately made sense to them. It was obviously not an idea that had occurred to them or if it had, it was quickly dismissed and never thought of again. These young women were committed not only to Naomi but also to the plan to return. They had to be wondering incredulously, what was Naomi thinking?

Surely We

Incomprehension, disbelief and bewilderment fill the faces of Ruth and Orpah. There is stunned silence, followed by an audible gasp and the heart-wrenching cry. "*Surely we.*" We are your family. You cannot abandon us. There are no others. You cannot mean you do not want us with you. You cannot mean you do not want us. We love you. Do you not know that? Does that not count? How can you be saying this? All this and more must have swirled around in the heads and hearts of Naomi's daughters-in-law in a mere half a second. It all became condensed into two painful words; *surely we.*

Will Return

The daughters-in-law are using the same word *return* as Naomi has used to tell the young women to *return* to their mothers' houses in Moab. The original idea of returning was to go back to Bethlehem with Naomi taking her daughters-in-law with her. The young women cling to this original meaning for return. Naomi had expressed to them that they would all return to Bethlehem. It is true that the young women had never been to Bethlehem and could therefore hardly return once again. Their "return" cannot possibly make any logical sense unless the closeness between Naomi and Ruth and Orpah is understood. As has been said, they had so closely identified with Naomi that her return to Bethlehem was their return also.

Now Naomi is telling them that *return* has changed direction and meaning. It now means going in the opposite direction on many levels. This includes a complete about face. Not only will they no longer set their faces towards Bethlehem, it also means that they will return to life in a pagan culture. It means that Naomi's return will no longer include them. Most of all it means that their returns will be in separate and separating directions.

With Thee Unto Thy People

As clearly as the young women felt that Naomi's return to Israel was inclusive of them, they did not feel a part of the Israelite nation. They had married Israelites but they did not feel that that made them Israelites. We see this in the fact that they refer to the people of Israel as *thy people.* And yet obviously knowing that they would be aliens in an alien land they felt so close and devoted to Naomi and loved her so much that this idea of alienation did not weigh very heavily with them. They had decided. Their desire was to go *with thee unto thy people.*

> *Ruth 1:11 "And Naomi said, Turn again, my daughters: why will ye go with me? Are there yet any more sons in my womb, that they may be your husbands?"*

And Naomi Said,

Naomi feels the full impact of her own words. She has had the briefest second to reflect and reconsider while her daughters-in-law have been questioning her with disbelief written on their faces. There is a chance to relent and change her mind once again. The strain on her heart is great. She is not happy to be parted from these her beloved daughters-in-law. She loves them. There are none dearer in the whole world to her.

They want to go. They really want to go with her. Look at their dear faces pleading with her. Once again Naomi must decide which way her daughters-in-law must take. How valid and how strong is her resolution concerning what is best for these lives that have been placed in her hands? *And Naomi said.*

Turn Again,

No matter what the temptation might have been at this point to keep her daughters-in-law with her, Naomi is resolute. They must go back to Moab. The Hebrew word for turn again and return is the same. The word in Hebrew is shub (or shuwb). It means to turn around or to return in a physical sense and also spiritually. After the children of Israel had left Egypt, there came a time of discouragement and they felt they should have never left Egypt. It got to the point of deciding to appoint a captain to lead them back.

> "And they said one to another, Let us make a captain, and let us return (shub) into Egypt."
> Numbers 14:4

Returning to Egypt was sheer rebellion not only against Moses, but with greater consequences against the Lord and all the plans He had for them (as a part of His covenant with Abraham and his son Isaac and Isaac's son Jacob.) Going back was rebellion against God. It is seen that the physical going back was closely tied to the spiritual. It is not only possible to *turn again* away from God but the opposite is also possible. Having left God, it is possible to *turn again* towards God.

Before the children of Israel enter the Promised Land, the Lord talked to them about what would happen if Israel turned away from Him. They would be driven from their land. He also promised to bring them back to their land if after they had been driven out they would turn their hearts to Him. He said:

> "And it shall come to pass, when all these things are come upon thee, the blessing and the curse, which I have set before thee, and thou shalt call them to mind among all the nations, whither the LORD thy God hath driven thee, And shalt return (shub) unto the LORD thy God, and shalt obey his voice according to all that I command thee this day, thou and thy children, with all thine heart, and with all thy soul; That then the LORD thy God will turn thy captivity, and have compassion upon thee, and will return and gather thee from all the nations, whither the LORD thy God hath scattered thee. Deuteronomy 30:1-3

Turning back towards God brought them not only back to a relationship with Him, it also brought them back in a physical sense. It brought them back to the Promised Land.

In her decision to return to the Promised Land, Naomi included her daughters-in-law quite naturally because they were her responsibility and more importantly they gave her life meaning. None of that has changed. What has changed along the way is Naomi's perception of what will be the life of her daughters-in-law in Bethlehem. The love of these devoted young women does not change her perception of the reality facing them. She cannot, she will not. She must not weaken and change her mind. They must go back. She must convince them that this is the best course, the only reasonable course open to them. She repeats it once more; she reiterates, *turn again.*

My Daughters:

In spite of her determination to send these young women away from her and back to Moab, Naomi admits at this crucial point how dear they are to her. For the very first time they are called daughters, *my daughters.* By this she is telling them that they could not be nearer or dearer to her heart than if she had given birth to them herself. She is telling them that to her they are her daughters. The bonds that hold them together cannot be broken. No matter what, they are her daughters.

For one all too brief moment, she is not a mother-in-law, she is a mother. Can this help them understand why it is so important for them to go back to their other mother? It breaks a mother's heart to give up her child. To have to make the decision twice is more than unbearable. This has to show her daughters how very hard this is for Naomi. At this very point of losing them forever, she speaks to them from her heart. They are not her daughters-in-law. They are her daughters-in-love. Will they trust her judgment because they trust her love?

Why Will Ye Go With Me?

With the question, *why will ye go with me?* Naomi must have lost them. What can she be asking? They were going with her because she wanted them to go with her. She had made this plan; it had been her decision. They had agreed with her because they loved her and wanted to go with her. They had made all their arrangements and had said good-bye, regretfully but willingly, to all their family and friends.

They had set out on the way and had talked of what different ones had said as they left, and had talked about what Bethlehem was like and the people and places they would see. At first it had seemed like a dream, but now the reality of living in Bethlehem had grown with each step along the way.

Why was Naomi asking this question? Did she have doubts about their willingness and true desire to go with her? Did she doubt their loyalty? What was the question behind the question? Did Naomi want the proof of their own words to reassure her? Although she loved them so much, did they return this same deep love? Were they willing to trust in this love no matter what? Had not all these questions been answered already? What can Naomi mean by this question of why? Before the young women can answer, Naomi goes on.

Are There Yet Any More Sons In My Womb,

Now Naomi is really puzzling. Of course she is not pregnant let alone being pregnant with twins. What can she be thinking? The answer is obviously, "no." What is she driving at?

That They May Be Your Husbands?

The young women's faces must have registered astonishment at what Naomi was saying. They knew Naomi was not pregnant. And even if she had been, why would she bring up such a thing? Surely Naomi did not think they would want to marry Naomi's fictitious twin sons. They knew she did not think any such thing. So what is her point? Before they can protest and ask any questions as to what can be the meaning of this silly question, Naomi continues.

> *Ruth 1:12 "Turn again, my daughters, go your way; for I am too old to have a husband. If I should say, I have hope, and should have a husband also tonight, and should also bear sons;"*

Turn Again

Once again we have the use of the words turn again or return (shub). They are the same word in Hebrew. Apparently, Naomi thought she had made the situation clear and that her daughters-in-law would understand what she was telling them and the unstated reason as to why they would be better off in Moab. They did not. This time she will make her point more emphatically. Even though she is going to dramatically clarify the situation for them, in order to brook no opposition, she starts with a command. *Turn again.*

My Daughters

Again, Naomi calls Ruth and Orpah her daughters. The command to turn again, while firm, is not cold. She tempers it with the use of the term daughters. This shows that in no way does she just want to get rid of them. She loves them dearly and out of this love and because of this love she must show them that they must return. It is her *daughter's* best interest that she is thinking of and not her deepest desires or wishes of wanting to keep them with her.

Go Your Way

Naomi is telling her daughters that the road back to Moab is the road that they must take. This is where they will find their best chance for a happy future. In saying *go your way;* she is saying that this is their destiny. It is not the life that she has been describing for them in Bethlehem. That was only an undefined dream of hers to keep them all together because she loved them so much. She had not given a great deal of thought to what her dream of their being together would mean in the lives of her precious daughters.

It had hit her suddenly and with stunning force that these daughters of hers had no future in Bethlehem except a dreary lonely life with an aging woman. That was not the future she wanted for her lovely vibrant daughters. They deserved more. They should have more. They would have more. She cannot show softness now. She cannot break down. Naomi gives another preemptory command. *Go your way.*

For

Finally, Naomi is going to make some sense out of all this. She is going to give a reason *for* why she is telling these young women to go back to Moab.

If I Should Say I Have Hope

Naomi is saying that if she were able to get pregnant things might be different. She had already reached an age where this was no longer a possibility or there would not be any "if" about it. In order to make the young women see the logic of her reason, in order to make her case, for urging them to return to Moab and have their mothers arrange a wonderful wedding with some nice young Moabite man, she was now going to pose a "what if".

If I Should Have A Husband Also Tonight,

Where is Naomi going with this? Ruth and Orpah know that there is no man in Naomi's life so why is she suggesting such a thing? There is no husband to be and further more there is no wedding night tonight or any other night in the future. Why would Naomi be proposing such a thing here in the middle of the road right after telling them they had to go back to Moab?

And Should Also Bear Sons;

Now this proposed scenario is really getting bizarre. Naomi is suggesting not only a wedding with some unknown man but also pregnancy and the birth of not just one son, but two sons, twins! Why is she repeating this idea of twins? This is getting more and more fantastic. Where is Naomi going with this ridiculous piece of fiction?

> *Ruth 1:13 "Would ye tarry for them till they were grown? Would ye stay for them from having husbands? Nay, my daughters; for it grieveth me much for your sakes that the hand of the LORD is gone out against me."*

Would Ye Tarry For Them Till They Were Grown?

Naomi is asking her daughters if they would wait for these improbable sons until they were grown up in order to marry them. She is asking it of these young women, who are the daughters of this family. Naomi knows that any baby born into the household would have not just one but three doting mothers. All three women would love these little boys and take joy in their little daily progresses into childhood and eventually into manhood. Each would thrill in the joys of all those precious "firsts" of baby and childhood; a first tooth, first words, and first steps. Yes they would tarry for them as mothers but how can Naomi be asking any other question? But Naomi has not finished this horrible imaginative scenario. Again, before the young women can protest, she continues.

Would Ye Stay For Them From Having Husbands?

The absurdity continues. Naomi has come to the final act of this unlikely drama. Are the young women willing to live out their lives with no hope at all of having husbands? Naomi has created an exaggerated impossibility in order to make an indelible point. There is no hope for marriage and a happily ever after for them in the country of Israel. Perhaps, as they reached that line of demarcation between two countries and two cultures, something occurred to Naomi. She had been familiar with life and living in Moab. There were different standards there. There was a difference in what was acceptable and what was not. Marriage with foreigners was apparently not a problem in Moab.

As the three women went along the way, Israel came in view, if not yet physically at least mentally. Naomi gradually became aware of her Israeli heritage and a more focused picture of life there. She had grave doubts concerning the acceptance of her daughters. She doubted if her widowed daughters would find husbands in Israel.

She could not allow them to be condemned to loneliness and no home of their own and no loving husband and no children. Naomi has tried her best to paint a picture of the impossibility of it all. Now will these young women see reason and act reasonably?

Naomi can think of no other way to make it more graphic for them. Out of pure unselfish love she has tried her best. This will not be easy for her. She does not want to lose her daughters but she must think only of them and what the future might hold for them. She loves them too much to hold on. Her nobility of character cannot be questioned even if her wisdom might be. She continues on a different note.

For It Grieveth Me Much For Your Sakes

Again, Naomi's thoughts are entirely for the benefit of her daughters. She is not grieving for herself and the lonely prospects that are set before her. She is not thinking about losing all that is left of her family. We do not know of any specific plans that she may have for her support. None of that matters to her. All her strength and energy centers on seeing her daughters cared for. The future she sees for them in Israel breaks her heart. It must not be allowed. It would hurt her even more than losing them. The thought of *for your sakes* is all that matters to Naomi.

That The Hand Of The Lord Is Gone Out Against Me

Naomi is making a very important confession. She is confessing that what has happened in her life has been the doing of the Lord and that she has suffered His chastisement. She is not blaming the Lord for being the prime cause of her woes. The Lord has clearly shown that He wants to bless His people and Naomi knows that includes her as an individual. She trusts the Lord as she has clearly shown in her prayer for her daughters. She has asked and trusts that the Lord will deal kindly in the lives of Ruth and Orpah. Naomi has asked the Lord to give them a secure future with a husband and a household of their own. She fully trusts the lives of her daughters to her Lord. She recognizes His jurisdiction in every area of her life and in the lives of her daughters.

She is acknowledging here that what has happened is against her personally and not against them, although they have had to also suffer. She does not say the hand of the Lord has come against us. She says against *me.* She is therefore acknowledging culpability.

We might well ask what ever has this loving mother done to cause the hand of the Lord to move against her. We cannot know. It is possible that her sin is not one of doing something that displeases the Lord but rather neglecting to do something very important in her role as a wife and mother. We have no evidence of her trying to convince her husband to return to Israel. He may have sinned against the Lord when the proposed sojourn became so comfortable that he continued there in Moab.

While doing something foolish is not necessarily sinful, knowingly continuing in foolishness is sin. As Elimelech's wife, (a wife by God's definition being a suitable and sufficient help), Naomi would have a responsibility to provide Elimelech with her wisdom on the subject of their continuing in Moab.

We also do not have any evidence that Naomi, when after the death of her husband became the head of the household, protested when her sons decided to marry Moabite women. While there was only strict prohibition against intermarriage with the various Canaanite nations, the reason for the prohibition also applied to marriage with the Moabites. The reason for no intermarriage with other nations was that other nations served false gods and once married to them, the foreigners would lead the children of Israel into idol worship and other abominations. The Moabites also worshipped foreign gods and therefore the same danger would be attached to marriage with them. The prophet Ezra also included the Moabites and others in the prohibition but he lived after the time of the book of Ruth. (See chapter nine of the book of Ezra.)

The sons married Moabite women without permission of their mother. When it became her sons' responsibilities, as heads of their new households, to move their families back to Israel, we do not have any evidence that Naomi urged them not to dwell in Moab. We do know that they dwelt there and they died.

While it is true that the account does not specifically spell out cause and effect, we do know that nothing happens by chance. Naomi certainly recognizes this fact and specifically says the Lord has dealt with her. She is telling her daughters that she is deeply sorry. What she has done has caused hurt to these daughters that she loves so much. *It grieveth me much for your sakes that the hand of the Lord has gone out against me*

> *Ruth 1:14 "And they lifted up their voice, and wept again: and Orpah kissed her mother-in-law; but Ruth clave unto her."*

And They Lifted Up Their Voice

Again we see them lifting up their voice. They are of one accord. All three of them feel the same in the deepest recesses of their hearts. They are so close that they are no longer heard as individuals. They are so attuned to one another that they have but one voice. This is a love of extreme rarity. It is a deep love between three women.

And Wept Again:

Bitter tears of inconsolable grief fell on the dusty road, forever marking this place as one of sorrow. They wept again and this time there was no momentary solace in a glimmer of hope. These were tears of finality. They would not question Naomi again. Naomi had vividly shown them that there was no hope for them in Israel. There were no husbands waiting for them in dreams of happiness. There were only years of poverty with an aging mother and after she was gone, then what? Naomi was right.

It was not that she did not want them with her. She loved them dearly as only a mother can love. They trusted implicitly in Naomi's love. Her reasoning, however, made sense. It would be better for them to go back. There was nothing ahead and everything behind. It made all the sense in the world.

There was no room for argument. Naomi was right. But how could something so right feel so wrong? To live without the constant love of dear Naomi could not be borne. And for Naomi to live without ever again seeing her loving daughters was also unbearable. How could she, how would she bear it? They held each other as if nothing would ever separate them as they stood in the way on the road to Judah, *and wept again.*

And Orpah Kissed Her Mother-In-Law

Lovely impulsive Orpah, the first married and so like her impulsive husband who had been always ready to grab life and run with it heedless of direction. Orpah was the first to recover her equilibrium. She realized that what Naomi was saying made eminent sense. Naomi had shown them that going back to Moab was their only alternative. Life was to be lived, not just endured. She loved Naomi dearly and Naomi had been the one to say she and Ruth must go back. There would be no blame.

Orpah knew she had to do it now, from this very spot or it would never be done. There would never be a second chance to return to Moab. She had to go now. There would otherwise be no life for her, no real life. Orpah wanted a life with a husband and babies. Who could blame her? Naomi certainly did not. Orpah knew she had no other real choice. So, as hard as it was, she decided to go back to Moab. She kisses Naomi good-bye and turns again towards Moab. We never hear of her again.

But Ruth Clave Unto Her.

There was something different about Ruth. She was not a second Orpah. The young women have always been seen as a pair. Never before had they been described separately. They had ever always been designated as a combination, a unit a duet. They were the daughters-in-law. It was only on their wedding day that they were named. They had often acted in concert; what one did the other did also. They were close in love for each other and had grieved together. Perhaps Orpah knew Ruth better than anyone else did. Orpah however, in this instance, did not wait for or suggest that Ruth go with her. It could be that she knew Ruth too well to even ask the question. Naomi had convinced Orpah to go back to Moab. She was already on her way. *But Ruth,* now that was a different story. She clung to Naomi like she would never let her go, let alone leave her.

> *Ruth 1:15 "And she said, Behold, thy sister-in-law is gone back unto her people, and unto her gods: return thou after thy sister-in-law."*

And She Said

Naomi speaks again. She has convinced Orpah to go back to Moab. Apparently, she did not convince Ruth with her illustration of what awaited Ruth in Israel. There must be some way of making this young woman see reason. Naomi tries again.

Behold, Thy Sister-In-Law

Naomi tries the "everybody else is doing it" tactic. She points out that Orpah, her sister-in-law, has gone back to Moab. She is appealing to the fact that going back made sense to Orpah and by extension it ought to make sense to Ruth too. Naomi further appeals to the closeness of the relationship of the two young women. In fact, Naomi does not name Orpah at all. She uses their relationship to identify Orpah and emphasize her point. She is subtly suggesting that Ruth can trust the love and therefore judgment of one so close. This is a whole new argument for inducing Ruth to return to Moab.

Is Gone Back Unto Her People,

To appeal to family ties is perhaps the strongest inducement of all. Naomi has used every argument she can think of and then she thinks of one more. She adds, on top of the points she has already made, the natural affection of loved ones still at home.

In going back to her mother's house, Orpah will resume her identity as a single woman. She will no longer be seen as a widow of Chilion but rather as an available woman, a prospective bride to someone else. Going back has effectively abrogated all she was in marriage. Orpah has gone back to life in Moab and life as an eligible daughter in her mother's house. Like Orpah, Ruth can have this too.

Naomi is also telling Ruth that she will be happier in her own country among the people of her birthplace. Naomi is, in effect, negating all of the Israelite religious observances in which Ruth most surely has participated. This is, in a real sense, a test of Ruth's decision to have become one with an Israelite, an Israelite who worshipped the one true God. How strong was Ruth's commitment to Mahlon's God, the God of Israel?

How strong was Ruth's sense of Moabite nationalism? If clear reason about the future had not swayed her and the idea of following the lead of her sister-in-law did not move her, would a renewed life with her family in the country of her birth persuade her to go back to Moab? Naomi comes up with yet another inducement to offer.

And Unto Her gods:

Naomi has fine-tuned and perfected the art of psychology in reasoned argument. She has tried to wear down opposition with point after point in order to get Ruth to return to Moab. It is not that Naomi sees Ruth as an opponent, just an immature young women not given to knowing what is best for her. Naomi has saved her most important argument for last. This is the clincher. This is the argument that will totally disarm Ruth. This is the one that will turn everything around.

Naomi knows that life is all about the God or gods you serve. As we have seen before, Ruth and Orpah have come to believe in the God of their husbands', the God of Israel. There could be no question of going back to other gods if they had not come to the point of placing their devotion to and trust in the God of Israel. This then is what Naomi is offering Ruth. She is offering Ruth a chance to turn her back not only on Naomi and their future life in Bethlehem, but also the God of Israel who could not be easily worshiped while on her own in Moab. There would be extreme pressure against such a stand, if not ostracism or worse.

It seems incredulous that Naomi would do such a thing. Why would Naomi set such a choice before a daughter she loves? It is as if Naomi has drawn a line across the road and was asking Ruth if she was sure she wanted to cross it. It seems like she has extended to Ruth every temptation possible and this is the greatest one of all. It reminds us of the time when Joshua called all the people together and gave them his farewell address. In part of his address he poses a question to the people and they answer him:

> "Now therefore fear the LORD, and serve him in sincerity and in truth: and put away the gods which your fathers served on the other side of the flood, and in Egypt; and serve ye the LORD. And if it seem evil unto you to serve the LORD, choose you this day whom ye will serve; whether the gods whom your fathers served that were on the other side of

> the flood, or the gods of the Amorites, in whose land ye dwell: but as for me and my house, we will serve the LORD. And the people answered and said, God forbid that we should forsake the LORD, to serve other gods;" Joshua 24:14–16

Naomi knew that there was nothing more important in life than the choice she has set before Ruth. She is plainly and simply asking Ruth to make a decision. Ruth must think very carefully. Unless she decides to serve the Lord, there can be no sense in continuing on with Naomi. This is the hardest question of all. It is not a question of physical or emotional preference. She is not being asked to choose between countries and families or of which she loves the most. The question is now a spiritual one. Will she serve the God of Israel or will she serve the gods of Moab?

Naomi is testing Ruth's commitment to God because it is surely to be challenged in the days and months ahead. It is one thing to give religious observance; it is another to have to place complete trust in God with one's life. There will no doubt be many times of trials ahead Ruth needs to settle this question once and for all if she is to have any peace in the midst of all that may come her way. She needs to decide now at this very time at this very spot on this very day. It is not something to be put off until some tomorrow. There are coming times when she will need a rock to stand on. She cannot survive in a morass of doubts and instability. Naomi is waiting. All of time and eternity waits.

Return Thou After Thy Sister-In-Law

Naomi has finished with all her reasoning and urgings towards a better life for Ruth. She now tries direct command. Once again, we have the use of the word shub, to return. It has now been used seven times. Three of those times pointed a return to Bethlehem and four of the uses refer to a return to Moab.

Naomi is using all of her authority. It will take a tremendous amount of strength of personality for Ruth to live in the foreign (to Ruth) country of Israel. It would have to be equal to the amount displayed by Naomi in her move to Moab.

Will Ruth now move in the direction of Moab? Will Ruth finally capitulate and return to Moab? Does Ruth have the same strength of character as Naomi? Will the first hint of it be displayed here on the dusty road? Will the book of Ruth end here or is there significantly more to her story?

> *Ruth 1:16 "And Ruth said, Entreat me not to leave thee, or to return from following after thee: for wither thou goest, I will go; and where thou lodgest, I will lodge: thy people shall be my people, and thy God, my God:"*

And Ruth Said

This is the first time we hear Ruth speak and through her words we will see into her heart and soul. Ruth will answer all that her mother-in-law has put before her and seals it with a vow. Over the years this passage of Scripture has often been used in wedding ceremonies because the sentiments of love are very profound and beautiful but (if possible) they are even more profound when we remember that these are not promises between couples on their wedding day but a declaration to a mother-in-law from her daughter-in-law.

Entreat Me Not To Leave Thee,

Ruth is begging Naomi to have done with all her reasoning, and enticements to a better life in Moab, and her demands for Ruth to return to Moab. Ruth has made up her mind and will not be moved. Her words could almost be read as a command of her own, were they not also a beseeching request.

This is the first statement on her own that Ruth makes, in the book of Ruth. (Both she and Orpah spoke together in questioning Naomi about the fact that surely they would both return with her to Bethlehem.) Careful note should be made of this opening statement of Ruth. It is important because it gives a close insight into her character. It also discloses what is uppermost in her mind and therefore most important to her.

She is most concerned with the possibility of being separated from Naomi. All of those other factors that Naomi has set before her to be weighed may be important to some extent. However, what is really most important to Ruth is her continuing in her relationship with Naomi. She knows that all those other considerations that Naomi has put forth might seem very important, such as a comfortable life and other people who care for her. They are not however, as important to Ruth as her relationship with Naomi.

Ruth knew that it is relationships that count most in life and she has a precious one with Naomi. It counts more than all the other considerations. What Ruth deeply feels and understands flows through her words. And so the first thing Ruth says, the preeminent thing she says is *entreat me not to leave thee.*

Or To Return

This is Ruth's second most important consideration. She does not want Naomi to insist on her return to Moab. She has decided to set her face towards Bethlehem, come what may, in order to continue her life with Naomi. She had been warned in strongest terms what that meant. There would be no husband. There would be no home of her own. There would be no children. There might not be a great deal of social acceptance. She and Naomi surely face poverty. She would be living with an ever-aging old woman who would probably have to be cared for at some point in time.

Ruth knew all that. Naomi had made it very clear. Still, she counted it as nothing. She knew that Naomi loved her and she knew above all that she loved Naomi. Everything else was sifted through this sieve and fell out. This is the eighth time we encounter the word shub (return) and the return is heavily weighted towards Moab (five towards Moab and only three towards Bethlehem). But eight is the number of new beginnings.

From Following After Thee

Ruth readily admits that Naomi is the leader and she is the follower. She does not want that to change. Ruth is talking here of following Naomi's lead all the way to Bethlehem. While she is talking specifically of following Naomi down the road, this will come to mean following Naomi's leading in other ways.

Naomi first took the lead or more accurately took responsibility for her daughters-in-law after the death of Naomi's sons who were the young women's husbands. Naomi made the major decisions including the decision to leave Moab and return with her daughters-in-law to Bethlehem.

It is also true that Naomi has taken the lead both emotionally and spiritually. Naomi has taught Ruth many things and will continue to do so when they reach the Promised Land. Most important of all, Naomi has taught Ruth the true meaning of love, the pouring out of self for another.

We see this in Naomi's decision to send her daughters-in-law back to Moab after her apparent epiphany on the way to Bethlehem. It would have been easy to keep her daughters-in-law with her. They loved Naomi and wanted to go with her. Naomi did not have to convince them to go. It was wonderful to have daughters-in-law who loved her so much. Just the thought of them all going their separate ways was devastating to them all. They did not just shed a few tears at the thought of separation, they wept. Yes, it would have been so easy to keep them but Naomi was selfless. Her thoughts were all for her daughters-in-law or as she called them, her daughters. She took no thought for herself.

If Ruth learned this kind of love through the example of her mother-in-law then perhaps Naomi had been too good a teacher for her daughter's own good. That, of course, was not the case. Naomi was a good teacher and it was all for her daughter's great good. Ruth could do no better than to follow after Naomi.

For Wither Thou Goest I Will Go;

Ruth did not need a gritty determination to shore up her resolve. Her decision had been made in her heart and no amount of reasoning with her mind would influence her decision in any way. It had been settled. Because of this she was able to speak with clarity and express exactly what were the settled facts. I *will go.* She has spoken and she will follow through no matter what. We see a firmness that is equal to and perhaps beyond Naomi's. There is nothing to be discussed. There is no disrespect in what Ruth is saying, just a calm unbendable resolution and purposeful will. *For wither thou goest I will go.*

And Where Thou Lodgest, I Will Lodge:

Ruth will not only follow Naomi, she will also stay with her. Ruth is reiterating the fact that not only will she follow Naomi's path physically (and we may also infer spiritually) but she is also going to live at the same address (again both physically and spiritually.) They will share the intimacy of family. Naomi is going to continue to be her mother. She expects Naomi to continue to love and care for her as she has done in Moab. Ruth is saying that our housing arrangements do not matter as long as we are together. It could be anywhere. The relationship that we have is what truly matters. It is our love that matters.

Thy People Shall Be My People,

Ruth is telling Naomi that she does not have to worry about her trying to maintain all that defines her as a Moabite. She will embrace all that is Israeli. She already has a good idea (granted not a full idea but a good idea) of what that means because of having been married to an Israelite and being a part of his family. She may have much to learn but it will not be a case of grudgingly learning what it means to be an Israelite, one of Naomi's people. She is going there, having already decided that *thy people shall be my people.*

And Thy God My God

Just as Naomi had left the most important question for last, so too, has Ruth left the most important answer for last. Ruth knew that it all centers on the God question. In life all other considerations pale in respect to this most important question. What about God? Will you give Him your complete love, devotion, and worship? Will you give your life to Him in total trust? Will you forsake all others keeping only to Him? Naomi needed to know the answers to all these questions before they could go on.

Ruth reassures Naomi. She has said that she loves Naomi and therefore will follow her. She has said that she will adopt the people of Naomi to be her very own. Now comes the most important question that needed to be firmly settled.

Beyond the question of where they will live and her relationship to the people they will live among, Ruth reassures Naomi by letting her know that she does not have to worry about this last question either. In saying, *thy God my God,* Ruth is not talking about adapting to Naomi's religion.

It may be possible that since, in the construction of the sentence with the conjunction "and" combining the two thoughts of *thy people shall be my people, "and" thy God my God,* that we could easily slip into the misconception that *thy God my God* means that Ruth is not yet a believer. That is however, not the point, let alone not true. It is not the point with good reason.

The conjunction is linking two relationships. There is the future relationship with the people of God and the future relationship with God Himself. It is not linking Ruth's future adoption of God's people to Ruth's future adoption of belief in God. For one thing, it would not make sense to say someday in the future I think I will adopt the religion of the people of Israel.

Belief in God is not the practice of a religion and

therefore something to be decided on, like whether or not to take a walk in the park tomorrow. One either believes or does not believe. (Practices such as prayer and worship grow out of belief but are not to be equated with belief.) A second reason this would not make sense is that Ruth already believes. What Ruth is actually doing is affirming her faith as so rock solid that it is already anchored in the future.

Thy God my God has nothing in-between because they are one and the same. *Thy God my God,* the one true God will be Ruth's God for all time and eternity. The living God of Israel is her God and because and only because He is already her God she can reassure Naomi about her fidelity in the future. The relationship already exists and will continue to exist. As we shall see, we not only have Ruth's statement, she will also make a vow.

> *Ruth 1:17 "Where thou diest, will I die, and there will I be buried: the LORD do so to me, and more also, if aught but death part thee and me."*

Where Thou Diest, Will I Die,

Ruth is telling Naomi that, this commitment will continue beyond the death of Naomi. Ruth will stand by her word until her own death which in the natural course of events will come a long time after Naomi's death. The spot, location, town, and country, in a word, "wherever" Naomi chooses to live, that is where Ruth will be situated for her whole life. In stating this, Ruth has settled all the rest with the finality of death, to bind herself to Naomi forever.

And There Will I Be Buried:

Ruth is saying that even after death, their mortal remains will continue together. What more can she say? Surely Naomi has to understand that her commitment is genuine and will last because it is not built on circumstances. Circumstances could change in anyone's life. Their relationship is built on love and trust, in God and love and trust in each other. This is what binds their lives together. This is why Ruth must continue on the way with Naomi.

The Lord Do So To Me,

Ruth now puts a death seal on all that she has said. Will Naomi now believe that she truly wants to go with her? Will Naomi now believe that Ruth wants her life to continue only with Naomi and Naomi's people, and especially with Naomi's God? She has taken a vow of death before Naomi and God. If all that she has said and all that she has promised is not kept, then she calls upon God to strike her dead. *The Lord do so to me.* This is no light thing that Ruth has done. She has not only put her future, committed to God and Naomi, on the line; she is also calling down severe judgment (death) upon her head if she does not live up to all she has promised.

And More Also,

What can be the "more" that Ruth is talking about when she says *and more also*? Would not striking someone dead be the ultimate and final punishment? Ruth knows it is not. There is eternity to consider. She knows that it is possible to be eternally outside of God's presence and this is a fate far, far worse than mere death.

If

"*If*" is a very small word with a very large duty. "*If*" is a fulcrum between the two ways: the way that follows closely behind and forever with Naomi, and the way that will part them forever. "*If*" is a conditional word and Ruth has placed the severest conditions upon herself.

Aught But Death Part Thee And Me.

The vow has been spoken with the conditions set. On the far side of being struck down dead is now the condition that it will not happen *if* Ruth stays forever with Naomi. Her lot has been cast and her fate sealed. Has she chosen wisely? The decision to stay with Naomi is no longer in her hands. She has given it back to Naomi with her entire life. What will Naomi decide?

> *Ruth 1:18 "When she saw that she was steadfastly minded to go with her, then she left speaking unto her."*

When She Saw

Naomi knew, in the depths of her soul, that the young women had to go back to Moab. In her mind, she had been convinced by all her reasoning power and by facing the "facts" that return was the only way for her daughters to find happiness. She was deeply saddened to see Orpah leave. It grieved her. Her only comfort, if you could call it comfort, was the fact that now Orpah had hope for the future. But Ruth had been difficult and made a desperate situation even harder. Ruth just did not seem to be able to see beyond the present. She was not being at all practical.

Naomi had tried to point out that Orpah saw reason. Orpah went back. Naomi had even tried to be a little forceful. Go. Return. It had not moved Ruth one bit. Now she had sworn this vow that was binding unto death. It was Naomi's turn to be astonished. Naomi finally *saw.*

That She Was Steadfastly Minded

Naomi saw that Ruth was more than determined. Hers was not a decision made in the logical recesses of her mind: her decision originated in her heart. Its direction could not be moved or swayed by any wind of change to suit the whims of situation and varying circumstances.

Since birthed from the heart it could not be changed by outward influences. Ruth's decision to go with Naomi was an expression of the love she had for Naomi. What Ruth has given to Naomi in this act of love is exceedingly precious and rare. It is even more rare when given to a mother-in-law. In all that Ruth had said, nothing could speak louder than this love. Naomi finally saw the consequences of this love. It made Ruth unmovable. *She saw that she was steadfastly minded.*

To Go With Her

The love that Ruth had for Naomi precipitated action as love always does. Love cannot help but express itself. It is an outpouring of the heart. By definition, love must be expressed or it is not love. Ruth's love for Naomi found expression in her desire *to go with her.*

Then

Then is one of those turnkey words. Everything that Naomi has decided for her daughters-in-law's future has changed in regard to Ruth because of this *then.*

She Left Speaking Unto Her

There is no longer any need for Naomi to argue her point or to plead with Ruth. Naomi sees what has motivated Ruth to want to continue with her. The subject of where Ruth will spend her future has been settled so *she left speaking unto her.*

Part Three – The Arrival in Bethlehem Ruth 1:19 to Ruth 1:22

Ruth 1:19 "So they two went until they came to Bethlehem. And it came to pass, when they were come to Bethlehem, that all the city was moved about them, and they said, Is this Naomi?"

SO

So is another of those little words with an enormous function. Before Naomi and Ruth could continue along the road to Bethlehem, there were certain issues that had to be resolved and settled. It had suddenly struck Naomi that taking her daughters-in-law to Bethlehem was not in their best interest. She was arrested by the realization of what these young women would actually face at journey's end.

So, she stopped right where they were in the middle of

their trip and told them they had to go back and why they had to go back. Orpah listened and reluctantly went back to Moab. Ruth heard what Naomi had said but it did not move her heart. She did not follow after Orpah to go back to Moab. She told Naomi that she was going with her.

Ruth did not try to argue with Naomi about the reasons why it was important for her to go on to Bethlehem. She just said she was going to go and she said it in emphatic terms.

Naomi realized there was no reasoning with Ruth. She realized that Ruth was unmovable and therefore stopped trying to persuade her. Because of all that had been said by Ruth, there on the road, half way between two worlds, Naomi was convinced and resigned. *So* she continued on the way back to Bethlehem.

They Two

From this point on, we no longer have Naomi as solely responsible for the decision to return. Neither do we have Ruth going with Naomi merely as a result of Naomi's decision to return to Bethlehem. We have two independent women, having made their own independent choice with their own free will. This is not to say that Naomi no longer feels responsible for Ruth or that Ruth no longer respects Naomi's position of authority in this family of two. That notion would be far from reality, as we will see.

It does mean that the choice to go to Bethlehem was freely made by each. The spiritual implications are also inherent in that their heading to God's promised land also meant heading towards a closer relationship with Him.

Went

The Hebrew word for went, (the verb to go,) is yalak. The first use of yalak in the book of Ruth is in the first verse when we see that a certain man went. He was leaving Bethlehem. The second time is in chapter one verse seven when Naomi went out of the place where she was in order to return to Bethlehem. It is also used in verses 8,11,12,16, and 18. Interestingly this is the eighth time it is used and again we truly see a new beginning in the lives of these women.

From this point of decision, both have recommitted, with a renewed and stronger purpose than ever, to return to Bethlehem. We see a new light and hope in their eyes. Now they truly know where they are going. *So they two went.*

Until They Came To Bethlehem

At this point in the story, they have arrived. From our position in Bethlehem, we have seen them coming. In many respects they were a long time coming. The family was gone from Bethlehem for ten long years but they have returned home. They have suffered many losses but they have come back. What was most important to their reaching their goal was for them not to stop or to turn back, but simply to continue *until they came to Bethlehem.*

And

The word *and* links two separate actions. It links the coming of Naomi and Ruth with the reaction to their coming on the part of the people of Bethlehem. The reaction gives us insight into the past of this family.

The lives of individuals always demonstrate many

character traits. But, lives are primarily a witness to the individual's response to God and His response to them. Herein is the meaning and within it, the purpose of the book of Ruth.

It Came To Pass

This phrase, *it came to pass,* was used in the first verse where we have it came to pass that there was a famine in the land and a certain man of Bethlehem-judah went . . .. It indicated, as it does here, that a certain amount of action and time has elapsed before we reach this point. Additionally, in this instance, we see clear cause and effect. Naomi's return has precipitated a response from the people of Bethlehem.

When They Were Come To Bethlehem,

The pace of the story picks up. We go from the women moving beyond the place of decision, directly to their reaching journey's end. They have arrived at their destination. They have reached Bethlehem. In reaching Bethlehem, is life as it was before, restored? Obviously, the answer is no. Things have radically changed for Naomi. She is no longer a wife and she has lost her two sons. Her former life can never be restored.

No one's life goes backwards or is restored. Naomi could not walk back into her past even though she has walked back to the place of her past. All Naomi can do, all anyone can do, is to move forward. Naomi and Ruth have moved forward to the place where the people of God dwell; and their God dwells among them. Naomi and Ruth now start their new beginnings in life. They do not have a new life but they do have a new beginning. It starts *when they were come to Bethlehem.*

That All The City Was Moved About Them.

Upon the arrival of Naomi and Ruth to Bethlehem, the first thing that comes to pass is that they are the center of attention and conversation. The whole city was talking about the return of Naomi with Ruth. Ten years is a very long time. A lot has happened in the daily life of the city. Weddings have taken place. Babies have been born. Familiar faces have passed away. There have been enough news worthy events to keep the most inarticulate talking for weeks upon weeks.

When the family first left, the whole city must have known about their moving to Moab. The event was a significant one and discussed by everyone. "Do you think they had a safe journey?" "I wonder if they found a place in a town that is friendly." "Do you think the Moabites in their area will give them a hard time because they are Israelites?"

After a time, friends and relatives would still wonder aloud about how the family of Elimelech was doing and how big the boys are now but life goes on and the thoughts for the family are less and less. Eventually, days and weeks and even years go by and there is no talk of Elimelech and Naomi and their boys. And now Naomi has returned with a young woman, a Moabitess, and Naomi has lost her husband and her boys.

All the city was moved about them. The Hebrew word for moved is hum (or huwm). It means to be excited, confounded, perplexed, stirred, disturbed, and to engender sympathy. Naomi and Ruth were "the talk of the town." It is doubtful that the return of a lowly, insignificant person would have been much noticed or commented upon. We have then the second hint that this family was a prominent one in the community. (The first hint was that they were Ephrathites.)

And They Said, Is This Naomi?

The question was not primarily one of identification. They knew this indeed was Naomi. What they were marveling at was all the changes in Naomi and her circumstances. Naomi looked different as anyone does after the passage of ten years, but the question went deeper because of what was written in the lines of her face.

The question was also much broader. What happened to Elimelech and Mahlon and Chilion? Who is this Moabite girl? What caused all the changes and circumstances in Naomi's life? Did she still have her faith in God after all that had happened to her? What will become of Naomi now?

> *Ruth 1:20 "And she said unto them, call me not Naomi, call me Mara: for the Almighty hath dealt very bitterly with me."*

And She Said Unto Them

Naomi openly speaks to one and all. She does not try to hide anything by quietly retiring and hoping her return will be unnoticed and unremarkable. She bravely faces her questioners and readily and willingly answers their questions. The first question she will answer is the question of most importance and really sums up and answers all the others. The question is simple and inclusive. The people want to know what has happened? Naomi answers with crystal clear clarity.

Call Me Not Naomi

The Naomi they all knew is no more. Too much has happened in her life for her to ever be the same as she was before leaving Bethlehem. The name her parents had given her, with the same fond hopes of all parents, no longer fits. Naomi has reached the lowest point of her life. Why call her pleasant when her life is anything but pleasant? Why call her comely and beautiful when tragedy has been etched on her face? She feels that the name of Naomi no longer describes her or her life. Under the circumstances, it was a bitter irony to call her Naomi.

Call Me Mara,

The name Naomi had everything to do with her visage and her nature. As it had turned out, her parents had picked out the perfect name for her. Naomi is now saying that her life has changed. She is no longer comely and beautiful. She no longer feels that the world she lives in is pleasant and that does not make her feel pleasant about it or herself. She suggests a more appropriate name would be Mara. So, she says, *call me Mara. Mara* means bitter.

For The Almighty

Naomi makes a full confession. She says that this is the doing of the Lord. It is a confession because everyone knows that the Lord delights in blessing His people but He will also chastise them if necessary. Naomi has already confessed to her daughters-in-law that the Lord has "gone out against me." Naomi knows that sometimes, bad things happen as a result of living in a fallen world. However, in her confession to her daughters-in-law she specifically says that God has moved against her as an individual. He has intervened in her life for a reason. It has caused her bitter sorrow.

Hath Dealt Very Bitterly With Me.

Here then is the reason for Naomi feeling she should be called Mara. It is not that, within her heart Naomi is bitter against God for what has happened in her life. She is not suggesting or confessing the idea that bitterness has taken root in her soul. She is reaffirming that the Lord has dealt with her and very harshly at that. She does not try to hide this and, in fact, is willing to wear the shameful label of someone with whom the Lord has had to deal bitterly. She is willing, for the rest of her life, to be identified in this way by assuming the name Mara. She is willing to be identified in this way because she also acknowledges the justification for having the name of Mara. In so doing she has confessed her sin before man and God. God will forgive her:

> "The Lord is long-suffering, and of great mercy, forgiving iniquity and transgression," Numbers 14:18a

This confession and God's forgiveness of Naomi's sin will allow the Lord to work in Naomi's life and to bless her but we do not want to get ahead of our story.

> *Ruth 1:21 "I went out full and the LORD hath brought me home again empty: why then call ye me Naomi, seeing the LORD hath testified against*

me, and the Almighty hath afflicted me?"

I Went

Naomi commences her revelation of what happened. With a statement acknowledging the fact that she left Bethlehem, Naomi admits that this is the starting point of all her troubles. It is the beginning of this ten-year disastrous drama and Naomi understands this. She does not say, my husband and I or our family went out; she says *I went out.* She takes personal responsibility for what has happened to her. This is an important part of her confession. She neither blames nor credits anyone with having influence upon her decision or actual subsequent going out. She does not seek to excuse herself in any way.

Out

Naomi and her family indeed went out, that is out of Bethlehem and outside of Israel. They went away from the land of promise; the land which God had given them. They went out of the land in which God had promised to bless them and be with them. Naomi sees this going out as a total explanation for all that has befallen her. She does not diminish this explanation by giving any other facts that could be seen as mitigating circumstances. She does not add other details, which might be interpreted as contributing to the problems and tragedies that she faced. There is one reason only. *I went out.*

Full

Naomi's use of the word full is all-inclusive. She had it all. She was a beautiful woman who had married well. She had had a wonderful husband and they were blessed with two sons who were their pride and joy. She had position in society and money to live comfortably. Life was definitely good. They did not leave Bethlehem because of poverty. They left because it seemed like the best way to hold onto what they had. Naomi went out *full.*

And The Lord

Naomi understands that it is the Lord who has acted in her life. He has always watched over her in love. Her absolute faith in Him has not been shaken and does not waver because of circumstances and adversity. It may be a simple faith but it is not simplistic. Her faith has the sleek aerodynamic quality that allows it to reach center target. There are no gyration-causing complexities.

Hath Brought Me Home Again

There is no doubt in Naomi's mind as to where her home is. Home is in Israel and more specifically in Bethlehem. Home was never in Moab even though she dwelled there. She credits her return to Bethlehem to the Lord. There is a shepherding quality in the Lord's leading her home, readily understood by all since being a tender of sheep was a common occupation in Bethlehem. Naomi was not speaking euphemistically or symbolically about the Lord's bringing her home. Naomi has always been straightforward and pragmatic. She is a no nonsense straight shooter. She says what she means and means what she says. The Lord *hath brought me home again.*

Empty

Naomi's use of the word empty is as exclusive as her use of the word full had been inclusive. She is using extreme opposites to make her point. Most people could remember what she meant by full. It brought back to their remembrance all she had when she left them. Now she is telling them that she is totally empty. She is empty physically, emotionally and spiritually. The starkness of her unembellished statement is a shock and profoundly disturbing.

If this could happen to Naomi who was a loved and respected figure in this community, then it could happen to anyone. Again, Naomi is in no way suggesting that the Lord was to blame. It was a relief to be home once again, full or empty. She is grateful that in her most desperate need that God has not turned His back on her and forgotten her. In spite of the fact that she has nothing to offer Him, He has still cared for and protected her. And above all, God has brought her back home again, even though she is *empty.*

Why Then Call Ye Me Naomi

Naomi is asking why the people insist on referring to her as if nothing has changed. Everything has changed in her life. She is not the person they knew and she rejects even the name she had before as part of what no longer exists. She lets them know for a second time that she is no longer the Naomi they all knew so well. She is someone entirely different and should no longer be called by the old name. Naomi gives reasons for justifying what she is insisting upon.

Seeing The Lord Hath Testified Against Me,

Everything that has happened, in the way of drastic change is easily seen by all. It is a testimony of the Lord's chastisement and no one in Bethlehem questions that. Naomi knows everyone can see the changes and she wonders at the fact that the people can go on acting like everything is the same. She believes it is a forgone conclusion in everyone's mind and they can all see that the Lord has testified against her. There is no need to go into further detail, as that would only cloud what is important here. The plain truth is that this is not a time for ignoring facts and this is not the time for misplaced tact or politeness, *seeing the Lord hath testified against me.*

And The Almighty Hath Afflicted Me.

Again, Naomi is confessing that God has punished her. *The Almighty hath afflicted me.* Her unhappiness, grief and hardship do not have simply natural causes, nor are they to be attributed to any particular person or persons. It is God's doing and He has dealt with her as an individual. Although calamity has come to the entire family, Naomi does not hide under the blanket of inclusion. She stands as an individual responsibly accepting the affliction as hers individually with the use of the singular pronoun me. The questions have all been answered in Naomi's confession. There is nothing more to be said on the subject. It is time to get on with life.

> *Ruth 1:22 "So Naomi returned, and Ruth the Moabitess, her daughter-in-law with her, which returned out of the country of Moab: and they came to*

Bethlehem in the beginning of the barley harvest."

So

Naomi had come to an end of the sojourn period in her life. The tale had been told. Naomi knew that sin remains in a life until confessed and forgiven. Therefore, even though she had decided back in Moab to change her physical location out of Moab and back to Bethlehem, it was not until she confessed her sin that forgiveness was possible. She was then in a position for God to work in her life all the blessings He had planned for her. *So* now, the move is behind her. *So* now, we can expect God to start something new in her life.

Naomi Returned

In this verse we again have the use of the word shub (return.) The word has come to represent a spiritual return as well as the physical return. Naomi's return is complete. She has returned to her spiritual inheritance.

And Ruth The Moabitess, Her Daughter-In-Law, With Her,

In the eyes of the people of Bethlehem, Ruth has two distinguishing marks of identification that define her. First she is a Moabitess. She is seen primarily as an unknown person of a nation with prohibitions against them. In order to maintain their hold on the Promised Land, the people have had to defend themselves from attack by other nations. Moab is one of these nations that, during the time of the judges, invaded Israel.

The Israelites also had specific commands from God concerning the people of Moab. Moabites were not allowed to be a part of the congregation (should they give up idol worship and turn to God.) This was only possible after ten generations because they had not let the children of Israel pass through their land when on the way to the Promised Land. Being a Moabitess was not in Ruth's favor as far as the people of Bethlehem were concerned.

Ruth's second mark of identification was the fact that she was the daughter-in-law of Naomi and it would have been evident that Naomi loved her very much. This, to some extent, may have weighed in Ruth's favor but to a larger extent her reception into the community was probably tepid at best.

Which Returned Out Of The Country Of Moab:

This constant refrain of return begins to seem overwhelmingly redundant. We get the picture. How many copies are needed? There is a reason for the repetition. Until the double use of the word return in this verse, the word always indicated intent, just as the staying in Moab had originally been intended as a sojourn, a short stay with the intent to return to Bethlehem. The intention never grew feet. The place of sojourn had become a place to dwell. Finally, in this verse we see the return, is no longer an ephemeral intention, it has become reality. The return has been accomplished.

Reiterating it for a second time in this verse seals it with glorious emphasis. There is completion. One of God's children has come home. It is a cause for rejoicing in heaven. It is a reason for us to also rejoice for the return of Naomi and Ruth (Ruth is included in the return.) It is always a relief to have a happy ending to a story. It is also a comfort. We somehow know that once again God has worked it all out. But this is not the end of the story. There is more, much more.

This eighth use of the word return marks a new beginning. The Biblical use of the number eight, to signal new beginnings, goes all the way back to creation. After God created the world and all that is in it in six days and rested on the seventh, the eighth day marked the beginning of a new week.

After Noah and his family entered the ark and God saw them through the worst storm the world would ever see, they stepped out to a new beginning for the world with eight people. When God gave the sign of circumcision to the Israelites, it marked the sign of the covenant that God had made with Abraham. Circumcision was to be done on the eighth day. (Our loving God has given little babies more clotting factor in their blood on their eighth day of life than they will ever have on any other day in their entire life.) Without going into a full discussion of circumcision, what is important here is the fact that on the eighth day it is done to show the beginning of life in a covenant relationship with God.

And so, here we have the eighth and last use of the word return. There is no longer a need to return. The return has been accomplished. We see a new beginning for Naomi and Ruth.

And They Came To Bethlehem

The return has turned into a coming. This is a change of perspective for them in that they were no longer leaving Moab. This is also true in a spiritual sense as well as physical. They came to Bethlehem and also to the Lord. They have arrived at journey's end.

In The Beginning Of The Barley Harvest

Spring, what a beautiful time of year to return to Bethlehem. There is promise in the air of rebirth and hope for the future. We know that in the far country, Naomi had heard that the Lord had given His people bread. In order to make bread one needs flour. Flour is made from grain. If Naomi and Ruth came at the very beginning of the harvest, after having heard about bread, it would seem to have been some time after harvest that word would have reached them.

It would have taken some time as well, to settle affairs, and say good-bye before leaving. The journey also took some time to accomplish. Therefore, the harvest that Naomi had heard about, actually happened in the summer before (or even the summer before that.) This would allow for a more extensive reason to spread the word of God's intervention on behalf of the people of Israel, because it would also include the wheat harvest that comes later. If the entire harvest season had been plentiful, the response of gratitude to God would have been so loud after a long famine, that it is no wonder Naomi heard it clear over in Moab.

It would also explain the ready acceptance of Naomi and Ruth into the community. The pinch of famine causes a lack of charitable feeling as everyone is concentrating on saving himself. The people had gotten beyond trying to save themselves in a desperate time of need. After many years of famine they had run out of self-sufficiency and desperately needed God.

God had heard their cry as they turned once again to Him. He gave them bread. There would have been renewed hope in the planting again; hope for another good harvest. The timing could not have been more perfect. As Naomi says, God has brought them back, and He has brought them back at the perfect time. He once again demonstrates in their lives that He does all things well.

Let us look for a moment at the significance of barley itself. Barley is the first grain to be harvested in the calendar year. The third festival to be celebrated each year in Israel was commanded by God to be the barley harvest, called First Fruits. (The first festival is called Passover. Passover celebrates the passing over of the angel of death in the land of Egypt. The angel passed over, that is, did not kill the first-born son in the houses that had the blood of a slain lamb sprinkled on the lintel and doorposts.) The second festival is the Feast of Unleavened Bread remembering the hasty exodus from Egypt with no time to let bread rise.

The Lord commanded that the children of Israel bring the first fruits of their crops to Him. (Exodus 23:19 and Deuteronomy 18:4) This also included the firstborn son to be dedicated to the Lord and the first born of animals given to Him, as well as the first wool of the sheep.

The people were to bring a sheaf of the barley harvest to the priest in gratitude for God's provision. The priest would take the sheaf in his hand and wave it before the Lord in celebration of what God had done for them. This had to be done before any more of the harvest could be completed.

> "Speak unto the children of Israel, and say unto them, When ye be come into the land which I give unto you, and shall reap the harvest thereof, then ye shall bring a sheaf of the first fruits of your harvest unto the priest: And he shall wave the sheaf before the LORD, to be accepted for you: on the morrow after the Sabbath the priest shall wave it." Leviticus 23: 10 and 11

The return of Naomi and Ruth at the beginning of the barley season had significance for their lives on both the physical level and on the spiritual level. In the natural, they came at a time when the abundance of provision could spill into their lives. On the spiritual level, it was a time to join the people in gratitude to God. Spring was indeed a beautiful time of year and it was only the beginning, *the beginning of the barley harvest.* There were more harvests to come.

Chapter Two

Part Four – Ruth Gleans in the Field of Boaz Ruth 2:1 to Ruth 2:4

Ruth 2:1 "And Naomi had a kinsman of her husband's, a mighty man of wealth, of the family of Elimelech; and his name was Boaz."

And Naomi Had A Kinsman Of Her Husband's

The first person, by name, that we learn about here in Bethlehem is a man who is Naomi's actual kinsman. He is a relative of Elimelech's. He is also related (not just connected) to Naomi because of her marriage to Elimelech. This is a little hard to understand today, unless we grasp the Biblical view of marriage in which two become one.

Naomi lived in a time when the Biblical view of marriage was a part of her culture. It was God's intention for a man and a woman to become one in every way, body, soul, and spirit. Woman, from the beginning back at the time of creation, is given to man in holy trust. A remnant of this idea holds over to this day in the father's "giving away" the bride. The woman became the groom's bride (belonged to him) and the couple became one. They became one in many, many ways. One of those ways was that his relatives became her relatives. *And Naomi had* indeed, become related to Boaz because she was wife to Elimelech.

The Hebrew word for kinsman, used here, is goel (alternate spelling gaal) and the meaning can also include, one who frees, redeems or helps. God says he is the one who freed the Israelites from bondage. He redeemed them. The whole book of Exodus is the story of this redemption and just one verse of many that states this is:

> "Wherefore say unto the children of Israel, I am the LORD, and I will bring you out from under the burden of the Egyptians, and I will rid you out of their bondage, and I will redeem (goel) you with a stretched out arm, and with great judgements:" Exodus 6:6

Naomi had a kinsman who was able to free them from their bondage of poverty. The question is not only how and why but most important of all, would he?

Naomi said before that God had stretched out His hand against her. Now that she has come back to Him, will God stretch out His arm to bless her?

A Mighty Man

Being a mighty man meant that he was a military man, a high-ranking officer, and had distinguished himself in battle. (As has been noted, the book of Ruth took place during the time of the judges when there were constant invasions of enemy troops into the land.) Being a mighty man also meant that he was a man of valor and honor and would be accorded great respect and stature. Mighty men held a high social position in the community. The Hebrew word for mighty is gibbon; it means powerful, warrior, and leader. God describes Gideon as one of these mighty men of valour.

> "And the angel of the LORD appeared unto him, and said unto him, The LORD is with thee, thou mighty (gibbon) man of valor." Judges 6:12

God himself is described as mighty (gibbon.)

> "For the LORD your God is God of gods, and LORD of lords, a great God, a mighty, (gibbon) and a terrible, which regardeth not persons, nor taketh reward:" Deuteronomy 10:17

Gibbon is also the word used in the great Shema that was quoted before and in part says:

> "And thou shalt love the LORD thy God with all thine heart, and with all thy soul, and with all thy might (gibbon.)" Deuteronomy 6:5

In modern-day Israel, everyone serves his country for three years starting at age eighteen. After that all men serve in the reserves for one to two months a year until age fifty-five and may be called up at any time to combat acts of aggression against Israel. At the time of the book of Ruth, Boaz was what may be termed as a very respected reserve officer.

Of Wealth Of The Family Of Elimelech

Boaz was a rich man. The traditional occupation in those days, in the area of Bethlehem, was to raise crops and tend flocks of sheep and goats and herds of cattle. It is obvious that the famine had not drained Boaz's resources to any great extent. He was wealthy. It is also obvious that the mentioning of his being a part of Elimelech's family, in the same breath, as it were, tends to emphasize the fact that Elimelech lost his portion of the family's wealth in Moab. Naomi has said that she went out full but has returned empty handed.

And His Name Was Boaz

We now have the name of this kinsman of Naomi. Boaz is the seventh and last person to be introduced in the story by name (other than those mentioned in the genealogical list.) His character has already been partially defined before we learn his name. He was a responsible man with a record of having served God and country with valor and honor. And significantly, as a clue to the rest of the story, we are told he is related to Naomi. His name means fleetness and strength. Have his parents chosen an appropriate name for him? We shall see.

> *Ruth 2:2 " And Ruth, the Moabitess said unto Naomi, Let me now go to the*

> *field, and glean ears of corn, after him in whose sight I shall find grace."*

And Ruth,

If we take the last word of the previous verse and the first two words of this verse we have "Boaz and Ruth". This may be mere coincidence (is anything mere coincidence?) but it does plant a subconscious link between the two. In all that has happened since Naomi's and Ruth's arriving we have not heard of or from Ruth. They two went (verse 19 of chapter 1) away from Moab and towards Bethlehem but it was Naomi who had returned to Bethlehem (verse 22 of chapter 1). Ruth was merely with Naomi. This was because, as far as the town was concerned, Ruth was only an appendage to Naomi's return and did not matter except for the fact that she was the person who was with Naomi.

The Moabitess

Ruth, in the minds of the people of Bethlehem, is defined and labeled. She is not seen primarily as the daughter-in-law of Naomi or the widow of Mahlon. She is seen primarily as a Moabitess and is therefore referred to not as Ruth but as RuththeMoabitess as if it were one word. This does not demonstrate an entirely positive attitude towards her. She is a foreigner. Being a foreigner perhaps makes her open to prejudicial suspicion to begin with. And worse, she is from the country of Moab, a country that, from the beginning, was not particularly friendly towards the people of Israel. No doubt, the people of Bethlehem will watch her closely before they make up their mind about her.

Said Unto Naomi

Once more, we will hear Ruth speak. There has been much excitement about the return of Naomi. Many people wanted to talk to her and they have so many questions. They were astonished. She looked so different and her circumstances had changed so drastically. How could this have happened?

And then there was this Moabite girl she had brought back with her. Why did she bring her back to Bethlehem? Wouldn't she have been better off among her own people? What kind of a person was she? How did Naomi feel about having a foreign daughter-in-law? Did she do things differently? Naomi was not going to allow any idols in her house was she? The questions went on and on. Finally, however, the dust settled. Finally things have quieted down; they are at last alone and Ruth has a chance to speak to Naomi.

Let Me Now Go

Ruth has decided to take practical initiative. She has bound herself to Naomi with the strongest bonds of love and this is again demonstrated in her desire to work for their sustenance. Ruth recognizes Naomi's authority over her in asking permission to go. Ruth does not see Naomi's authority over her as translated into Naomi's responsibility for her in their very basic need to eat.

These women are poor and there is not a whole lot they can do to better their situation. Naomi's greatest desire had been to return to Bethlehem, the scene of her birth and life before the family left to sojourn in Moab. She had come home. There really was no future for her and she had now seen all the old familiar faces and some new ones too. She had accomplished her goal. She had fulfilled the family hope to someday return. There was nothing more in life for her, no future. It was all over. The road led her back to Bethlehem and the road ended here. It was time to give up but ironically there was literally nothing to give up. There was nothing left of her life before and no longer anything left to live for. Naomi had reached the end.

And what about Ruth? Dear Ruth. She had freely chosen to come to this; Naomi's dead end and now she must eek out an empty existence. Naomi had tried to warn her but she would not listen and now there was no hope for either of them. Ruth stood before Naomi, eager to set forth. Poor Ruth, she was a good girl, a loving girl but she just did not understand. There was no place to go.

To The Field,

Ruth was asking for permission to set out from the town of Bethlehem to go to the field area that surrounded the outskirts of the group of dwellings and other buildings that constituted the city. The Hebrew word for field is sadeh and means a fertile field; a level place or an expanse.

To Glean

Naomi and Ruth had arrived in Bethlehem at the beginning of the barley harvest. Many hands were needed to gather in the grain. There is timing involved. The grain must reach perfect ripeness and must be harvested in dry weather. As the men and women scythed and gathered the grain, on a fine day in late spring, the laborers would invariably drop some of the stalks with their fully ripened heads of grain. These, and the grain standing in the corners of the field, were to be left for the poor and strangers (foreigners.) A scythe is swung in a circular motion and thus one would have to go back over some of the same area in order to cut down the square corners of the field being harvested. By the commandment of God, these corners and the stalks dropped were to be left so that even the poor and foreigners would be provided for. Picking up what was left was called gleaning.

> "And when ye reap the harvest of your land, thou shalt not wholly reap the corners of thy field, neither shalt thou gather the gleanings of thy harvest. And thou shalt not glean thy vineyard, neither shalt thou gather every grape of thy vineyard; thou shalt leave them for the poor and stranger: I am the LORD your God." Leviticus 19: 9-10

In order to strongly impress upon the people of Israel that they should obey this commandment, God reminds them who is speaking. It was so important to God that He boldly and purposefully puts His signature on it. He reminds them that this is the LORD speaking this commandment. God cares very much about the poor and the stranger or foreigner. In His blessing of abundance to Israel, He has included provision for the poor and foreigner.

Ruth was aware of this commandment and practice of the Israelites and wanted to help in providing for the needs of Naomi and herself. In wanting to glean, Ruth is not only acknowledging their situation of being poor, she is ready to do something about it and she does not wait to be told. She takes initiative. The Hebrew word for glean is laqat. Laqat also means to pick up, to assemble, to collect, and to gather. When the children of Israel were in the wilderness after leaving Egypt they murmured against Moses and Aaron saying that they should have stayed in Egypt where at least they had not starved.

> "Then said the LORD unto Moses, Behold, I will rain bread from heaven for you; and the people shall go out and gather (laqat) a certain rate every day, that I may prove them, whether they will walk in my law, or no," Exodus 16:4

Gathering the manna in the wilderness was a test of following God. Gleaning in the field must have also been a test for Ruth. Bending over all day was not easy work. It would have been very understandable if Ruth had misgivings about her decision to accompany Naomi to Bethlehem just as the Israelites questioned their decision to leave Egypt. There is not the slightest evidence or inkling that Ruth questioned her decision. She looked forward and not back. Her willingness to do the lowliest job, to glean, opened the door for God to bless her and Naomi through her.

Ears Of Corn

The ears of corn that Ruth wants to glean are not maize. Corn was the generic word used interchangeably for grain in general. We have already been told that it was the time of the barley harvest. Corn as we have come to know it was a product of the New World grown by Native Americans and had not been introduced to Ruth's area of the world. Ruth wanted to go out and gather the stray stalks with heavy heads of barley grain.

After Him In Whose Sight I Shall Find Grace.

Ruth did not know where she was going to be able to glean. Apparently, not everyone followed the commandment of the Lord to allow gleaners onto their field. She trusted that she would find someone who would let her glean in his field. Ruth does not assume that she has any legal rights. This is because it may or may not be a part of the owner's policy to follow the law of God and allow gleaners access to the droppings of his harvest.

The Hebrew noun for grace is chen. It is based on the verb chanan. Chen means to show kindness or favor and grace. (It also means aesthetic beauty, charm and loveliness.) Chen is also used in the sense of the strong showing pity to the weak. Naomi has said that Ruth has shown much kindness not only to her but also to her son. We will see if the same kindness that Ruth has shown will be shown to her.

And She Said Unto Her, Go, My Daughter.

Naomi sees the need for Ruth to go out and glean with the poor. She and Naomi are poor and need food to eat. Naomi is ever practical and without any discussion between them Naomi again, with all the force of brevity, directs Ruth to go. It is reminiscent of the time that Naomi told Ruth and Orpah to "Go". This time she is directing Ruth to the fields of Bethlehem to find sustenance rather than to the fields of Moab.

The last time Ruth was spoken of, she was called Ruth the Moabitess as if Moabitess were her surname. Naomi has not adopted this appellation given to her daughter-in-law. As she had done on the road, she again calls her daughter. Just because Naomi has resumed life in Bethlehem does not mean that she sees Ruth any differently than she came to see her in Moab. She loves Ruth. She calls her daughter.

> *Ruth 2:3 "And she went, and came, and gleaned in the field after the*

reapers: and her hap was to light on a part of the field belonging unto Boaz, who was of the kindred of Elimelech."

And She Went,

Ruth set out purposefully. Naomi had not only given her permission, she had said to go and so Ruth went. This time she follows the instruction to leave Naomi and sees it is a going that will hopefully benefit them together as the other going would not have done.

And Came,

We see Ruth arriving at a barley field where, with hard work, she will be able to gather up stray stalks of grain that have been dropped or overlooked by the harvesters. She *had come* to Bethlehem and the start of a new life in the Promised Land. This is where God literally dwelled among His people. These are the people whom Ruth now claimed as her people even if they were hesitant to receive her as one of their own.

Now she *came* to another new start in life in a barley field. She was willing to start at the bottom, so to speak, on the lowest rung of society. She was not ashamed to associate with the poor and lowly. Whatever her position had been in Moab no longer counted here in her present situation. She *came* to do an honest day's work in order to support Naomi and herself.

And Gleaned In The Field After The Reapers:

Ruth found a field where she was allowed to glean. All the area around Bethlehem that was able to be cultivated was called the field and various residents of the city owned portions of it. Beyond the cultivatable fields were hills that had suitable vegetation for Bethlehem's sheep and other livestock. Ruth, with permission, started to glean. As has been said, gleaning was not easy work. It was back aching and itchy as little bits of dried barley leaves clung to sweaty skin. Ruth toiled long and hard for a pittance of grain, finding only the stray bits that were left as she *gleaned in the field after the reapers.*

And Her Hap

A hap is something unplanned and unlooked for. Ruth's hap was an unlooked for circumstance in her life that she did not plan or contrive. It was purely *hap*penstance.

Was To Light On A Part Of The Field Belonging Unto Boaz,

Ruth had come to the cultivated area outside of Bethlehem. Many properties were being harvested of the ripened barley. Ruth chose one at random and was allowed to glean after the reapers had gone through the field picking up the barley that had been cut down. As it turned out, the field that she had chanced to choose was a field that belonged to Boaz.

Who Was Of The Kindred Of Elimelech.

We have already heard of Boaz and of his relationship to Naomi. We now learn that there are more relatives and he was just one of them. There may have been more than one Boaz in Bethlehem but the one whose field that Ruth happened to light on was a field belonging to this member of Elimelech's family. It is a curious coincidence that out of all the fields, Ruth should happen to pick one belonging to a rich relative, although she does not yet know that he is a relative. She will be sure to tell her mother-in-law about all that happened when she returns home again with her gleanings.

> *Ruth 2:4 "And, behold, Boaz came from Bethlehem, and said unto the reapers, The LORD be with you. And they answered him, The LORD bless thee."*

And, Behold,

We go from seeing Ruth working hard at gleaning in a field to an unexpected STOP and "take notice" event. Behold is a "heads up look at this" kind of word. Everyone is doing his job and everything is going along smoothly when something of great note takes place. The flow of events is interrupted and everyone stops and looks up. This is an important event and everyone in the field is aware of it.

Boaz Came From Bethlehem,

We have heard of this person but now we are actually

going to meet him. This is our first live encounter so to speak. It is apparent that Boaz's coming was an event of which note should be taken. It is a "look at this" moment. Boaz, the man who is mighty and is wealthy, the owner of this field being harvested, has come out from Bethlehem. He apparently wants to see how the harvest is going. He obviously has not taken part in the work so far today and has hired many to work for him.

We are again being made aware of his position of rank that commands respect. This is recognized simply because attention is directed to the fact twice. First there is the arresting of attention by the use of the word behold as if a headline were in the making. Then there is the newsworthy event that Boaz came and not only came but with the added information that here he was making a special trip from Bethlehem. He obviously had other things to do but had taken time out of business in Bethlehem to see how the work was going forward in the field.

And Said Unto The Reapers,

Boaz has come and everyone is aware of his coming and who he is. He has their attention even though they probably continue to work. He speaks to them. He does not speak through the foreman or anyone else in charge, thereby placing himself on a pedestal above his laborers. He communicates directly with them.

The Lord

These are the first words we hear out of the mouth of Boaz. This is significant in and of itself apart from what is being said. It defines what is uppermost on his mind; his first thought. It is also significant because it tells us something important about Boaz. It gives us our first impression of his character. His first words are *The Lord.* He puts the Lord first in the words that emanate from his mouth. This allows us to realize that the Lord is first not only in his speech but also in his heart and life. This is a shining example to those around him and to those for whom he holds responsibility.

Be With You.

Upon seeing the reapers, Boaz's first words were a greeting and a prayer for them. *The Lord be with you.* He does not ask first about how the harvest is going. He does not comment favorable about the weather. His first concern is for the reapers. He demonstrates his trust in the Lord and prays that the Lord will be with them.

In a broad sense, God was with the children of Israel throughout their wilderness experience in a pillar of fire by night and a pillar of cloud by day. He has promised to dwell with them in the land. So, in a sense He is with them.

What Boaz is praying is that God will be with them in the sense that He is a part of their daily individual lives. This of course happens when they open their lives to Him as individuals. God wants to be a part of each person's life. Each reaper needed to place his trust in God and God would be with him. Boaz could not desire for all in his employ a greater hope and blessing than *the Lord be with you.*

And They Answered Him,

The reapers respond freely and without fear of presumption or disrespect to Boaz's position. They respond to him and to his profound prayer and greeting with a greeting and a prayer of their own. The feeling between the reapers and Boaz is warm and open. They freely give back an answer to what he has spoken to them.

The Lord Bless Thee.

The reapers are all of one accord in their desire for Boaz. It is their desire that he be blessed of the Lord. It would seem that Boaz already has been blessed of the Lord. He has position and wealth but the reapers wish him further blessing. Even if these greetings had been of the most casual sort (and there is no indication that this is the case) the words have still been spoken. A blessing has been spoken on the part of both Boaz and the reapers to the benefit of each other. As God is their witness to the beneficent desire on both sides, He has also been called upon to make good these desires. Will God respond? Have His plans already been put in motion, on their behalf, without their awareness?

Part Five - Ruth Meets Boaz and They Speak in the Field. Ruth 2:5 to Ruth 2:18

Ruth 2:5 "Then said Boaz unto his servant that was set over the reapers, Whose damsel is this?"

Then Said Boaz Unto His Servant That Was Set Over The Reapers,

Boaz speaks again. In a general way he has recognized everyone and more than given them a friendly greeting. Boaz speaks again. This time he is talking to a particular individual. This individual is a servant of Boaz. He is the servant that has been set over the reapers. He is an overseer, a manager, a foreman, and is in charge of the people who are reaping the barley. This particular servant is on the staff of Boaz, which probably includes many servants. He has been chosen because of his administrative ability and knowledge of what the job entails, has been chosen for this job. Boaz now has a question for him and expects he will have the information that Boaz is seeking.

Whose Damsel Is This?

Boaz has obviously noticed that there is someone in the field that he does not recognize. There is no question in the servant's mind of whom Boaz is speaking. There is not more than one unknown young lady in the field. This indicates that Boaz knows everyone else. He is not an employer who has no knowledge of those who work for him. These are not mere people without an identity as far as he is concerned. He knows his workers and probably quite a bit about each of them. They are a part of the people of his community and they are familiar to him.

There is one person here, however, that he does not recognize. He expects he can get some information about her and her identity from his servant/foreman whom he expects has a handle on all that is happening in his field. If anyone knows who she is it would be this man. And so, he asks, "*Whose damsel is this?*"

Interestingly, Boaz does not come straight out and ask who is she? He suggests by the wording of his question that the young lady must be connected to someone. She did not just come walking down the road from a distant unknown place to glean in his field. Beautiful young women with a quiet air of dignity do not just materialize out of nowhere. Boaz thought he knew everyone in Bethlehem so where is she from, how did she get here and with whom is she connected?

Boaz is curious about this mysterious stranger. He wants to know her background and more about her than just a mere name would reveal. He inquires of his servant. And as he hoped, the servant has the answer.

> *Ruth 2:6 "And the servant that was set over the reapers answered and said, It is the Moabitish damsel that came back with Naomi out of the country of Moab:"*

And The Servant That Was Set Over The Reapers Answered And Said,

We are again told that the servant that Boaz is talking to is a man who is in charge of the harvest of this field that belongs to Boaz. Saying something twice gives it emphasis. No one interrupts the conversation between these two men. No one interjects his eager contribution of explanation about the beautiful young stranger. No one presumes that he knows more about her unaccountable presence than the man in charge. No doubt, everyone in the field knows about her by now. This servant knows exactly who she is, where she is from, why she is here and to whom she is connected. He is able to not only answer the question but is willing and eager to go further and fill in all the details about this beauty that has appeared in Boaz's field.

It Is The Moabitish Damsel

Amazingly, that is all the servant feels he needed to say. *It is the Moabitish damsel* says it all. He assumes that this identification of the woman by way of her nationality is all that Boaz needs, to place her in context. We have been told that all of Bethlehem was moved about the event of Naomi's return and "all" must mean exactly that – all. Everyone knew the story of Naomi and had wondered and talked about the great loss that had occurred in her life.

Naomi's story, of course, includes a Moabite, as by now everyone knows. There would have, undoubtedly, been much speculation about this Moabite daughter–in–law. Natural curiosity would have to be satisfied. She was talked about and watched very closely. Everything she did was open to speculation, evaluation, and interpretation; her every move was noted. Her dress, the way she carried herself, what she says and how she acts, especially towards Naomi, is all observed, noted and judged. Yes, everyone knows about the Moabitish damsel and the servant safely assumes that Boaz does too.

That Came Back With Naomi

The servant definitively places the Moabite damsel within the precinct of Naomi's story of coming back. This Moabite damsel, moreover, is a part of Naomi's coming back. She came with her to Naomi's rightful place, to the place where Naomi belonged and to the people to whom Naomi belongs. They did not know that the full account of Naomi's coming back has only begun. The full story of coming back is yet to unfold.

Out Of The Country Of Moab:

The servant is not being redundant because while it is true that Naomi came back and Ruth came with her, it is also true that they came out of Moab and all that Moab represents. It is another reminder that Naomi has returned to the place where the God of Israel is worshipped and away from the gods of Moab. They have come out, totally out of the country of Moab.

> *Ruth 2:7 "And she said, I pray you, let me glean and gather after the reapers among the sheaves: so she came, and hath continued even from the morning until now, that she tarried a little in the house."*

And She Said, I Pray You, Let Me Glean

The servant tells Boaz that Ruth has presumed nothing. She does not assume that because it is the law of God that she should be allowed to glean in any field in Israel, that she might just go ahead and glean. She asks permission of the servant in charge.

It may be significant that the servant set in charge does not report to Boaz that he gave the Moabite damsel permission. This may indicate that there is no need to report giving permission because it is the policy of Boaz to follow the laws of God. The servant must know that it is the policy of Boaz to allow gleaning in his field and therefore the servant sees no need to indicate that he gave his permission.

What was significant is that Ruth asked. This shows something of her character. She is humble and careful not to give room for offense. She sees herself lower than a servant without resentment and yet is independent and not looking for charity. And so she asks, *pray let me glean.*

After The Reapers

In a word, (after) Ruth is shown willing to take left-overs. She finds value in what little the reapers have over-looked or dropped and left laying on the ground. She follows behind the reapers and works hard to gather the little that is left from the great bounty that belongs to some-one else. She is appreciative of the slim amount that has been left behind and is now her portion. What joy it was to find the single head of barley grains hidden and left behind among the cut off stubs of barley. Her eyes searched keenly back and forth for the next one that may even be hidden under the stubble now pressed down and trodden over by the feet of the reapers.

Among The Sheaves:

Ruth asks permission to gather among the sheaves. Ruth walked among the fat tied bundles of barley stalks that stood in the field with their heads bent over, heavy with grain. The harvest had been plentiful as God blessed his people graciously in giving them abundance so that they would have enough to eat and make bread for a year until it was time to harvest again.

In a very tangible way, Ruth was walking among what represented some of the wealth of Boaz. As a farmer, his bank account, so to speak, his income is tied up in the crop he produces. This was a field of plenty and all Ruth asked to do was to gather with patient effort that which had been left behind.

So She Came

This then is just about all that the servant can tell Boaz in the way of new information about Ruth. It had impressed him that Ruth had asked permission. It was the first thing he wanted Boaz to know about Ruth. The rest everyone knew. Asking permission was a gracious thing to do and showed everyone that she was willing to work for herself and Naomi. It also showed that it is likely that she knew something about the laws of Israel. She, after all, had been the one to ask Naomi if she might go and glean. Naomi had not suggested it to Ruth. Ruth has a real interest in her new country and she is learning more every day. She has learned that God makes provision for all that put their trust in Him. He wants to bless them.

And Hath Continued Even From The Morning

Ruth started in the morning and has worked steadily. This is one more thing that the servant is pointing out to Boaz. It is certainly in her favor in the eyes of the servant of Boaz. A hard working person is universally admired. The servant is impressed. He lets Boaz know that she is not a slacker; she is a diligent worker.

Until Now,

It is now sometime in the afternoon. Morning has passed and the laborers have already accomplished much. Boaz's visit coincides with the time everyone takes a break. His visit will not interrupt the work going on. He can now make a good estimate as to how long the whole job will take and he will catch his foreman at a time when he is not as busy and can talk to him without taking him away from his job. The foreman tells Boaz that the young stranger has worked all morning until now without pausing for a break or stopping to take a rest.

That She Tarried A Little In The House.

Ruth has come to tarry a little and take a rest. She has come with the others who have been working in the field. The house is actually a shelter, perhaps without sides, set up for those working in the field so that the workers might take a break out of the sun. It is also a place for necessary items needed in the harvest and the workers can leave extra garments that they no longer need once the chill of the morning wears off.

Up until this point, Ruth has worked steadily, bending over to pick up the few stray stalks of barley. It would have felt good to straighten up and stretch for a time. Ruth shows great sensitivity in wanting to be with the harvesters. She is showing that she identifies with them, is not above them. (Simple shyness could have been interpreted as superiority.) It is true that in coming to the shelter she opens herself up to an opportunity to be questioned but perhaps she realizes that this is only to be expected.

She identifies with these, God's people and wants them to know it. She has made a commitment to Naomi as all can see from her presence in the field and her willingness to work hard for the benefit of them both. She now demonstrates that she also identifies with these people of the Promised Land. She wants them to know that she has not only committed herself to Naomi but she has also committed herself to become one of them. As she has made a vow before God, these people are her people. She demonstrates it here as she works among them and rests among them. Let the questions come. She has taken the opportunity to show herself by deed, now she will have the opportunity to show herself by word. What may seem threatening is actually an opportunity and Ruth is ready for the challenge. *She tarried a little in the house.*

> *Ruth 2:8 "Then said Boaz unto Ruth, Hearest thou not, my daughter? Go not to glean in another field, neither go from thence, but abide here fast by my maidens:"*

Then Said Boaz Unto Ruth,

For the first time, Boaz speaks to Ruth. The difference in their stations in life is enormous. Their situations could not be more unequal. He was rich. She was poor. He was an Israelite and she was a Moabite. He had great position in the community. She had come in the back door, so to speak, and only tenuously had a low position by way of having once been married to an Israelite. He had the respect of the community. She was a stranger who was unknown, let alone the question of having earned any respect. There would have been those who saw her less than zero, decidedly in the negative as an extra burden to Naomi who already had more burdens than most. And now here is the mighty man, and wealthy besides, not only noticing her, he is actually speaking to her.

Hearest Thou Not,

Boaz is saying in effect, do you hear me? He is not actually asking about her hearing acuity. He wants to know that she is listening to what he is about to say to her. He is making sure that he has her attention. He is going to say something that he wants her to be clear about. He is emphasizing that he is going to say something important to her and he wants her to take him seriously. He is not about to make a casual comment such as may be made to anyone and quickly forgotten. He makes sure she is not only listening but will take to heart what he is about to say.

My Daughter?

Boaz is not claiming paternity. He is using the term daughter as a way of expressing his position in relationship to her. He is far above her in the social setting of Bethlehem and that is a part of what he is stating. The endearing and close term of daughter takes away the sting of pointing this out to Ruth while maintaining the authority one such as a father would have.

Assuming the authority of a father also gives Boaz the right to tell Ruth what she may and may not do. And further, it also expresses the kind of concern he will show in the same comfortable relationship of a father to his daughter. There is somewhat of a spirit of noblesse oblige here.

The law states that, the stranger and the widows and orphans, are to be cared for by the community. There is acknowledgement on the part of Boaz in his actions towards Ruth, that as someone the Lord has so richly blessed, he has responsibility towards her. She is definitely poor, a widow and a stranger in the land. Boaz has already shown strength of character. His speaking to Ruth is in keeping with his already demonstrated character.

Go Not To Glean In Another Field,

Boaz is giving Ruth a direct command. This is the fourth time that Ruth is told to go and this fourth go is negated. The first time she was told to go was in chapter one, verse eight – go, return, back to Moab. The second time was also in chapter one verse twelve, - go your way (back to Moab). The third time was in chapter two, verse two – Naomi told Ruth to go to the field.

Now we see the fourth time Ruth is told to go and then the go is negated, *go not*. In the first three instances, Ruth was to go (back to Moab twice and then to the field) in order to help her find a better future. Now the idea of going is negated by Boaz. Is this an, oh so subtle hint, that Ruth has found her better future so there is no longer the need to go? The story continues.

As a free agent, Ruth may go anywhere she pleases. If she finds a field that will allow her to glean more grain than she has been able to find in this field, she is perfectly free to go and glean there, (provided the owner allows her to glean.) Ruth, no doubt, knows this. Why then would this person be telling her not to go and glean elsewhere? What is it to him where she gleans? What does he mean by giving her orders even if they are spoken so kindly and showing apparent concern for her in taking notice of her, a poorer than poor widow?

Neither Go From Hence,

Ruth must have felt a little taken aback, if not totally shocked that the mighty Boaz had addressed her, and it was probably written all over her face. Just in case she does not understand, Boaz restates what he has said to her. Ruth is not to go from this field. This is the fifth and next to last time that Ruth is told to go and it too is negated. Twice in this one verse, Ruth is told she is to go no more.

Rather than now clearly understanding what Boaz is about, Ruth must have been more bewildered and more mystified than ever, as to his intentions towards her. Why is he so insistent that she stay here? What can he mean by it?

But Abide Here Fast By My Maidens:

Boaz has now told Ruth what she must do and what she must not do. He has told her that he does not want her to leave the precincts of his field and he wants her to *stay by my maidens.* These young women who are helping in the field with the harvest are a part of Boaz's staff. They work for him. This indicates that Boaz had a large household if these young women could be pulled away from their regular duties in order to help with the harvest. He is an employer and responsible for many people.

Ruth must be wondering more than ever what this all means. Is Boaz suggesting that she fit in with his maidens? Is he going to hire her on a full time basis because she works so hard or because he knows her story and feels sorry for her? How are the other young women going to react to having her foisted among them? There were so many questions. Maybe Naomi could sort this all out for her. Maybe Naomi could explain it all. She would have to wait until she returned home, but now it was time to get back to work.

She knew that her tired muscles would be complaining to her loudly tonight. They were already tired but she must work harder than ever. All those around her were obviously watching her. That did not matter so much. What was more important was the fact that she and Naomi were in great need. She needed to do her best in order to provide for them. There was no one else. In some ways she felt so alone. No one could understand what she had been through and what she had lost and how much it had cost her to come. The cost counted less than nothing because she loved Naomi so much, but she was a little tired and hungry.

> *Ruth 2:9 "Let thine eyes be on the field that they do reap, and go thou after them: have I not charged the young men that they shall not touch thee? And when thou art athirst, go unto the vessels, and drink of that which the young men have drawn."*

Let Thine Eyes Be On The Field That They Do Reap,

Boaz is giving further instructions. Again, Boaz is not speaking entirely in a literal fashion. Ruth must of course look down at the ground in order to spot the heads of grain. What Boaz is saying is that Ruth should not look at other fields with the idea of finding a better place to glean. She should not let her eyes wander, thinking that the grass is greener, so to speak, in another field. She should not think that she would find another field where more grain has been overlooked. No other field will give her a better chance for finding even more grain than she is finding in this field belonging to Boaz. He is saying, "Don't even think about it. Stay here."

And Go Thou After Them:

Boaz adds a further stricture. He is saying, in effect, that if your eyes have already gone there, if you have already thought about going elsewhere, do not do it. Do not put feet to what may already be an idea. Boaz knows that the thought comes first before an action. He has said do not even think about it. Now he is adding, if you have thought about it, forget about it. Do not give life to the thought by taking action. Do not do it.

This is the sixth and final time that Ruth is given instructions about going and the third time going is negated. Any idea that she might have of going has been strongly negated. Clearly there is no more having to "go."

Have I Not Charged The Young Men That They Shall Not Touch Thee?

Boaz now gives Ruth incentive to conform to what he is asking of her. And, he was asking. His telling her not to go elsewhere may have sounded like a command but there are several reasons why this is not the case.

First, both of them know that he has no jurisdiction over her. She is a free agent and can go where she likes. He cannot force her to stay exclusively in his field. Second, he has called her my daughter. This may have been a figure of speech that he used all the time with everyone but it did imbue his directive with subtle concern and authority. And now, third, he feels it necessary to inform her that he has gone out of his way to make her experience here in his field free from unwanted attention from the young men in the field.

He may or may not have done this as a general practice concerning any young lady in his field. It may have been his practice to warn the young men not to give unwanted attention to any young lady in his employ. It seems, however, that in Ruth's case Boaz has made an overt and direct effort to warn the young men. This is seen in Boaz's reassurance to Ruth that he has told the young men not to touch her. The reference to touching was not necessarily physical. This is especially true of the period. Touching can include teasing, taunting and even suggestive looks. Boaz has told the young men in so many words to "lay off."

He tells Ruth about what he has done on her behalf in hopes that this will convince her to stay with his maidens in his field where she will be protected. Ruth has no one to protect her and Boaz has seen this and has offered her protection. Boaz did not have to do this. He was not particularly responsible for Ruth. He has gone out of his way to show Ruth favor. Ruth had told Naomi that she wanted to glean in a field belonging to someone with whom she would find grace. She has indeed found grace, that is, unmerited favor, from Boaz.

And When Thou Art Athirst,

Boaz shows Ruth even more courtesy and concern. He realizes that the work of gleaning is tiring and that she will at some point become thirsty. He is acknowledging her need for a drink and is going to offer help.

Go Unto The Vessels, And Drink Of That Which The Young Men Have Drawn.

The young men who work for Boaz have drawn water from a well and have filled vessels. This water has been provided for all the workers so that they may have a drink when they become thirsty. Boaz tells Ruth to feel free to drink of this water when she feels thirsty even though she is not working for him and he is in no way responsible for her. This is a kindness shown to her that reflects his awareness of her needs and again is a gracious act. Ruth once again has found grace that she desired in her field of "hap."

> *Ruth 2:10 "Then she fell on her face and bowed herself to the ground, and said unto him, Why have I found grace in thine eyes, that thou shouldest take knowledge of me, seeing I am a stranger?"*

Then She Fell On Her Face And Bowed Herself To The Ground,

Ruth is overwhelmed and overcome. For Boaz to even recognize her existence in life is totally unexpected. She falls down before Boaz as if he were the most powerful king in the whole world. She prostrates herself before him. She did not just courteously bow in deference to his mighty position in life. He is not a king but on the other hand he is one of the important, if not the most important, man in Bethlehem. She has perhaps grasped this fact, through conversation with the workers in this field where she has been gleaning.

At any rate, she recognizes his station in life and she did not understand what was happening or why he should speak to her. Ruth knew that this was not in any way what she had expected when she left home with Naomi's permission and set out to find a field in which she would be allowed to glean.

And Said Unto Him, Why Have I Found Grace In Thine Eyes,

Ruth had desired to find grace in someone's eyes so that

she would have the opportunity to glean some barley in his field. This is certainly not a grandiose wish. All she wanted was a little thing, a little grace. She was not asking or hoping for much.

She had expressed this to Naomi. Naomi had thought it likely that her desire would be granted and so gave her permission. God granted her desire beyond all hopes.

Ruth's humility is shown here in that she did not desire or even less expect the notice of such an exalted person as Boaz. Ruth acknowledges her extreme lowly position in life. She humbles herself before Boaz in the posture of lowliness.

If she did not have it before, she has since learned Naomi's acceptance of reality. Her station in life may have been very different in Moab. There is even belief in Hebrew tradition that she was the daughter of a king. Whatever the case may have been in Moab, it is not the case now. She demonstrates that she faces life with the same grip on reality as Naomi does. She is not, however, struck dumb with speechlessness because of her present position in society. She asks Boaz a direct question. *Why have I found grace in thine eyes?*

That Thou Shouldest Take Knowledge Of Me,

Ruth feels that it is extraordinary that Boaz should even take notice of her existence, let alone speak to her and go beyond just speaking. He has taken steps to ensure her safety and the need for a refreshing drink whenever she is thirsty. In her mind, this accommodation towards her is unusual. She cannot understand why he is going to such lengths and so she asks for an explanation.

Questioning someone who is lofty in comparison to her after having bowed so low in acknowledgement of his position, shows that Ruth has a dignity of her own and is no one's sycophant. She readily understands that what Boaz has done is not in the norm. It is, in fact, extraordinarily unusual. She wants an explanation and asks it immediately and directly of him.

Seeing I Am A Stranger?

Ruth voices another very good reason for why Boaz should choose to completely ignore her. This reason goes beyond the fact that she is only another poor person who has so little that she needs to glean the droppings that have accidentally been left behind in their insignificance.

The second reason for ignoring her might be an indication of at least part of the reception she has experienced here in Bethlehem. By reason of being a stranger or foreigner, Ruth feels it would be only normal that Boaz would ignore her. She indicates this in a very direct way to Boaz. She lets him know that she cannot understand his kindness towards her, seeing she is a stranger. She feels that just the opposite of kindness would be normal and certainly more understandable. She openly points this out to him and requires an explanation.

> *Ruth 2:11 "And Boaz answered and said unto her, It hath fully been shown me, all that thou hast done unto thy mother-in-law since the death of thine husband and how thou hast left thy father and thy mother, and the land of thy nativity, and art come unto a people which thou knewest not heretofore."*

And Boaz Answered And Said Unto Her,

Boaz is not so high and mighty that he feels her question is impertinent and therefore he would be justified in refusing to answer her. There is no indication that he even felt that she was out of line in the way she poses the question. He could have easily felt that she has judged him to be automatically prejudiced towards strangers (foreigners) because of the way she had been treated by others of his countrymen. This is not the case with Boaz. He takes her question and its implied judgment in stride. He is more than willing to accommodate her and answer her question. His doing so, and promptly, shows that he is not offended and has a predetermined good reason for what he has done. It is also clear that in his mind, the steps he has taken are not merely a generous whim but are carefully thought out, and to his way of thinking, quite reasonably justified.

It Hath Been Fully Shown To Me,

Boaz is stating, that not only has he heard about Ruth, but, he has heard about her at length. It is not known who gave Boaz his information but he asserts that it is quite complete. Probably he has heard the story from many friends and relatives. Naomi and Ruth had been the talk of the town, instant celebrities as it were. Every scrap of information was talked about and assessed with eagerness. It was shared over and over. Ruth could not be aware of how much interest the community took in her. Boaz has heard the reports and has drawn his own conclusions about Ruth before he ever met her.

Most of what has been said must have been very positive. There could be only one original source for information about Ruth and that was Naomi. Naomi has told everyone that Ruth is a loving blessing to her. She has told everyone that Ruth was not only a wonderful wife to Mahlon but also kindness itself to her and she is grateful and loves Ruth dearly.

The stories that have flown around Bethlehem were numerous and Boaz has heard a great many of them. He says *it hath been fully shown to me.* He shares with Ruth what is being said about her and what he has heard. Ruth must have been aware that she was a topic of conversation but it is doubtful that she knew the full extent of the conversations that centered around and about her.

It must have been a bit of a shock to learn that he knew about her, and knew quite a bit. He is someone who obviously had much more important things to be concerned with and to occupy his mind than a mere impoverished foreigner.

First he takes notice of her and then he goes out of his way to show unusual kindness to her. Now he was saying he knows all about her. It is no wonder that Ruth has asked her question in unbelieving amazement. Boaz shows understanding of the situation and takes the time and makes the effort to explain it all to her.

He starts by saying he has heard all about her. Ruth understands somewhat that there is bound to be talk but to have an exalted stranger say he knows all about her was not something she is prepared for. It must have been written on her face because Boaz does not give her a chance to register understanding but continues to explain his reasons for what he has done.

All That Thou Hast Done Unto Thy Mother-In-Law

Naomi has told everyone much about Ruth. She has not only detailed one or two incidents of kindness to Ruth's credit, she has had much to share. Her conversation has been full of the praises of Ruth. In her evident gratitude to Ruth and to God for giving her Ruth, Naomi has not dwelt on all her grief and destitution. She has chosen to dwell on expressions of love for Ruth and all the ways both great and small that Ruth has demonstrated her love for Naomi. Naomi has left the dead behind in Moab and is more interested in telling everyone about her unbelievably wonderful daughter-in-law. The whole city is filled with these stories of Naomi's and it is apparent that Boaz has heard a great many of them.

Since The Death Of Thine Husband

Boaz is making an important point. There would have been ample reason for Ruth to have cordial relationships with her mother-in-law during her marriage but Boaz points to Ruth's relationship with Naomi after the death of Mahlon. In using the encompassing word all, Boaz is stating that he has heard of the many acts of kindness that Ruth has shown to Naomi when she no longer had any obligation to Naomi.

It is a testimony to Ruth's character and Boaz is conscious of it. Ruth had had a great loss too. One might expect her to indulge in self-pity and excusably to have thought only of herself and the tragedy that had befallen her. She might legitimately have felt that it was time to expect others to identify with her grief and to minister to her. No one would have blamed the beautiful grieving young widow.

Instead of sealing herself off in the wrappings of widowhood, Ruth chose not to dwell on her own needs but to look beyond self to the needs of her dear mother-in-law with understanding, comfort, and love. She gave of herself to her mother-in-law. She totally sacrificed her life and all hope for her future on the altar of complete guileless love.

Boaz had heard of this and in his heart he honored Ruth for what she had done. When he had the opportunity of meeting her it was an easy choice for him to look out for her in this simple way of a few words to the young men, offering a drink of water, and a direction to her to stay in his field with his young maidens where he had control of what happened on his property.

And How Thou Hast Left Thy Father And Thy Mother,

Boaz realizes and states to Ruth that he knows that she has left behind in Moab her father and her mother. He knows to leave father and mother is not easy for anyone. There would never again be a chance to see or speak to those dear loved ones again.

It could not have been an easy decision. From the point of leaving, and forever after, they were to her as dead. Ruth's grief was compounded by her decision. Boaz not only knows this, he honors her for the sacrifice she has made. He knows the decision to set forth with Naomi cost her dearly and he speaks of it now. He speaks directly to her soul. He voices understanding about this costly and rare act of love she has shown towards Naomi.

And The Land Of Thy Nativity,

It is hard to know how difficult it was for Ruth to leave forever the land of her birth. There are very strong ties to the earth where one grew up. In those days, the likelihood of Ruth ever returning to the familiar landscape and scenes of childhood would have been very slim.

Boaz may have been far away from home when fighting battles. He therefore probably knew at least a little, what thoughts of home meant when home was left behind. Boaz speaks of the fact that Ruth has given up her homeland for the sake of Naomi. There is every indication of understanding in his words that mention her leaving the land of her nativity and surely even deeper understanding in his eyes.

And Art Come Unto A People Which Thou Knewest Not Heretofore.

In reciting to Ruth all that he knows about her, Boaz saves perhaps her most difficult sacrifice for last. Boaz realizes that it must in some ways make Ruth feel so alienated and alone among people who are equally foreign to her as she is to them. Boaz says that in coming to Bethlehem, Ruth is coming to a people she has up until now not known. She does not know their customs and culture, she does not know what is important to them as a people, she does not know their views about government and worship of God, and she does not know their views of life and its meaning.

When Boaz says she has come to a people she does not know, for the most part, he is right. What Boaz has not taken into account is that she was married to an Israelite and has come to accept at least some of the Israelite traditions but more importantly she has come to trust in the God of Israel and that one thing makes all the difference in the world.

Trusting in the Lord will open the door to loving His people as well as knowing and loving Him more and more. All the rest, in the way of culture, can be learned. By trusting in the living God, Ruth has a guide for the path set before her. She has been through so much in her short life. She has placed her trust in the Lord and that gives her a security and a peace for all her tomorrows. She has proved that she knows how to be steadfastly minded once she makes up her mind. Could Boaz see all this as he looked into her beautiful countenance? His next words indicate that he did.

> *Ruth 2:12 "The LORD recompense thy work, and a full reward be given thee of the LORD God of Israel, under whose wings thou art come to trust."*

The Lord Recompense Thy Work,

Boaz speaks a blessing upon Ruth. He prays, that the Lord will pay her back for all that she has done for Naomi. In his blessing, Boaz starts with *the Lord.* He is not giving her a casual God bless you. He is placing in God's hands his desire for her blessing, knowing that it is the Lord that ultimately provides all blessing. Boaz's blessing goes beyond generality. He desires that the Lord recompense Ruth; pay Ruth back, give her compensation for her work.

And A Full Reward Be Given Thee Of The Lord God Of Israel,

A reward goes far beyond recompense or compensation of fair payment for work done. In his use of the word full, Boaz expresses his desire to see her receive a reward that could not be larger. He wants the reward to be full, to complete capacity. The Hebrew word for full is shalem and it is an adjective based on the verb shalam. Shalem means lacking nothing, entire whole, and perfect (as in full measure, just measure).

> "But thou shalt have a perfect (shalem) and just weight, a perfect (shalem) and just measure shalt thou have: that thy days may be lengthened in the land which the LORD thy God giveth thee." Deuteronomy. 25:15

It is this kind of full that Boaz wants for Ruth, perfect fullness as only a perfect God can give. Another insight into this word shalem comes from the description of the stones from which the altar of God was to be built. They were not to be chipped away by iron tools, but were to be whole (shalem) stones. Each stone would be slightly different, but whole, with a beauty of its own in the Lord's service.

> "Thou shalt build the altar of the LORD thy God of whole (shalem) stones: and thou shalt offer burnt offerings thereon unto the LORD thy God:" Deuteronomy 27:6

This passage is speaking of the altar that was to be built on Mount Ebal. This actual altar has been found just a few short years ago. Waiting thousands of years, it is the oldest Biblical archaeology site found to date. It dates clear back to the time of the Israelites entering the Promised Land. This is before the time of Ruth. What is most interesting is that the stones of the altar, which is huge, are all uncut stones just as God had instructed that they should be; perfect with nothing missing.

Undoubtedly, Boaz would have known about this altar and how God had required it to be built of whole, not hewn, stone. In the desire of Boaz for Ruth to have a shalem reward there is the thought that perhaps Boaz desired, for her, a life that was full and perfect and that nothing would chip away at her peace as iron on stone would do.

Under Whose Wings Thou Art Come To Trust.

What a beautiful metaphor of protective care this man uses. He has the soul of a poet and is very tenderhearted. The picture Boaz presents is one of a mother bird and her little ones who find refuge, safety, comfort, and warmth under her wings. Boaz is saying that he knows that Ruth has come to trust in the God of Israel and goes to Him for refuge.

The Hebrew word for trust is chacah. Besides trust it also means to have confidence in and to hope in. It is also a place to seek refuge. In military strategy a high defensive position gave military advantage such as Masada where the Israelites in later years held out against the mighty forces of Rome.

Spiritually speaking, going to God is the place of refuge. We still carry over this idea today in that in time of war places of worship are spared and are considered places of sanctuary and refuge.

Some years after the time of the book of Ruth, King David wrote:

> "God is our refuge and strength, a very present help in trouble." Psalms 46:1

It was this verse that inspired Martin Luther to write his famous and beloved hymn, "A Mighty Fortress Is Our God."

> *Ruth 2:13 "Then she said, Let me find favor in thy sight, my lord; for that thou hast comforted me, and for that thou hast spoken friendly unto thine handmaiden, though I be not like unto one of thine handmaidens."*

Then She Said,

Ruth is not so much intimidated by the position of Boaz that she cannot speak to him again. What he has said to her has not grown out of his duties and responsibilities. He has spoken as a fellow believer in God and she answers him on that level. It is on this level, with her indomitable strength of character and faith in God that she is able to speak freely to him. Behind her words we also see, once again, that this woman has gentle dignity.

Let Me Find Favor In Thy Sight,

Ruth did not understand why Boaz had taken notice of her and then shown unusual concern. She asks him a very direct question, expecting an explanation and he gives her one. He says he is not only aware of all she has done but is also extremely impressed, very favorably impressed. He desires that she will have it all be rewarded by the hand of God.

Ruth expresses her sense of gratitude in humility. She hopes that she will be worthy of all that Boaz has desired of the Lord on her behalf. In saying, *let me find favor,* she is saying that she hopes that she will in the future gain his approval in all that she does. She wants to continue to live up to his expectations and evaluation of her. She does not exclaim, that of course she loves Naomi and will continue to do her best for her sake. She is not offended that obviously she has been the topic of discussion. She is not offended that she has been judged (even though that judgment is favorable.) She does not demand the source of his information or even ask what kind of reports he has heard about her. None of that forms a part of her response to him. She is humble. She takes what he has said to heart concerning his desire that she be blessed of the Lord and embraces it with all her heart.

My Lord;

Ruth, in calling Boaz lord, is showing that she understands his position in relationship to her. She is showing respect towards him. She was being very polite. It is interesting, however, that there is another case of a woman calling a man lord. Sarah loved and respected her husband Abraham very much and called him lord.

For That

The words *for that* mean, because, or for that reason. Ruth is saying that she wants to live up to the assessment that Boaz has made of her character. This is important to her because of what he has done for her. She realizes he can have no idea of how much his demonstration of kindness means to her and how his words have spoken to her heart almost to the point of being overwhelming.

She is desperately grateful and her extreme words and posture of lowliness in her bowing to the ground show how keenly she has felt the separation from family and homeland even though she may not admit it to herself. It is almost as if she has practically fallen apart over the kindness Boaz has shown her which in all reality is not so very great. Her response is intended to demonstrate how grateful she feels, but it more graphically shows the state of her mind and heart.

Thou Hast Comforted Me,

Ruth wants to continue to keep the good opinion of Boaz because he has comforted her. Boaz has expressed that he understands all that Ruth has done for Naomi. He truly understands how hard it was to leave her family. He understands how hard it was to leave forever the country of her birth and entire life up until this point. Just because she has done it willingly, with great love for Naomi and trust in God, did not make it easy. It made it possible, not easy.

Ruth has found comfort and encouragement in what Boaz has said to her. She knows in her heart that he understands. Her heart is overflowing with gratitude. Her appreciation is deep and helps to predicate her desire to continue down this difficult path she has freely chosen in love. The Hebrew word used here for comfort is nacham. It means literally to take in breath forcibly such as to gasp or pant. It can mean to be sorry or to pity. It can also mean to comfort or console as someone who is mourning is comforted by friends and loved ones, or as a mother comforts her child who has hurt himself. It means to have compassion.

Accepting consolation creates a change in a person. As Ruth accepted understanding and consolation from Boaz she was comforted. A lovely story of finding comfort is found in the very romantic story of Isaac and Rebekah. (See Genesis 24)

Isaac had mourned very deeply over the death of his loving mother. His father Abraham loved him very deeply too and determined that Isaac needed a wife. How a wife was found is an exciting and lovely story and in the end Isaac is comforted with his loving sympathetic wife.

> "And Isaac brought her into his mother Sarah's tent, and took Rebekah, and she became his wife; and he loved her: and Isaac was comforted after his mother's death." Genesis 24:67

And For That Thou Hast Spoken

Ruth adds to her reason for wanting to continue in the

good opinion of Boaz. She tells him how much she appreciates his speaking to her. He could have easily overlooked her or ignored her once he knew who she was. He chooses to speak to her and even communicate to her that he knows all she has done. He has not only heard about her but the reports of her have impressed him very much and he says so. His willingness to speak to her has impressed Ruth very much too. She also forms a favorable impression of him and tells him why.

Friendly

There is a great deal of difference between speaking as a wealthy and prominent citizen as well as employer/owner of this harvest and speaking on a friendly basis. Boaz has spoken in a friendly way with the concern of a friend. The Hebrew word for friendly is leb and means from the heart. It is seen in such common English expressions as wholeheartedly, heart and soul, and a heartfelt expression.

We attribute the deepest emotions as coming from the heart. "To the very heart of the matter," means to the core of the matter. Ruth was expressing this idea of Boaz speaking from his heart to hers, a close heart to heart exchange.

Unto Thy Handmaid,

Ruth is not a servant to Boaz or even working for him. She is making the point that she is no more in rank than one of his handmaidens. It is a polite and courteous way of stating her position in life compared to his. She is pointing out that his speaking to her is not in the usual way, it is unexpected, and to her, a little incredible.

Though I Be Not Like Unto One Of Thine Handmaidens.

Ruth cannot understand why Boaz has shown kindness to her and has also chosen to speak to her as a friend. It adds to her perplexity in that she is not of the nationality of his handmaidens. She knew it was easy to see that she was not one of them and that she obviously stood out among the others. In Ruth's way of thinking, this did not work to her advantage; quite the opposite. It was therefore more inexplicable than ever as to why Boaz should have spoken to her as a friend. Heretofore, this has not been her experience and it therefore makes her wonder why he has done so.

> *Ruth 2:14 "And Boaz said unto her, At mealtimes come thou hither, and eat of the bread, and dip thy morsel in the vinegar. And she sat beside the reapers: and he reached her parched corn, and she did eat, and was sufficed, and left."*

And Boaz Said Unto Her,

As Boaz speaks to her again, Ruth could have reasonably assumed that now she would have an explanation. Now she would be able to understand what motivated Boaz in his taking notice of her, his provision for her comfort, and his speaking in such an understanding and friendly way. If she did expect to have this mystery cleared up for her, she was to be disappointed. There was no explanation forthcoming. Boaz speaks of something different and if anything adds to his mysterious behavior.

At Meal Times Come Thou Hither, And Eat Of The Bread,

Boaz speaks with further kindness. They were standing in the house prepared for the workers of the harvest, when Boaz began to speak to Ruth. He continues speaking to her and tells her that at mealtimes she is to come back here to eat and she is to eat of the bread that has been furnished for the laborers. Bread, of course, is Biblically very symbolic. Ruth has come to Bethlehem, the house of bread and now we see that bread has been provided for her without any labor on her part. It is a gift; a gift of the staff of life. And Boaz, whom she realizes, owes her nothing, has provided yet again and yet more for this stranger. Why, she must have wondered, why?

And Dip Thy Morsel In The Vinegar.

Again, Boaz adds to his kindness and provision for Ruth. He invites her to dip her piece of bread in the vinegar. Vinegar was made from grape juice that has been allowed to ferment. Grapes, the fruit of the vine, also have great Biblical significance and symbolism. The grapevine is a Biblical symbol for the nation of Israel. Grapes were part of the richness promised to the Israelites once they entered into the Promised Land.

As the spies came back to report about the land before the nation went up to enter it, the spies brought back an assortment of fruit to demonstrate to the children of Israel the bounty of the land. The bunch of grapes (one bunch) was so large that it took two of the spies to carry it attached to a pole and carried between the two of them.

"And they came unto the brook of Eshcol,

> and cut down from thence a branch with one cluster of grapes, and they bare it between two upon a staff; and they brought of the pomegranates, and of the figs." Numbers 13:23

God's blessing to the Israelites was great. The fruit of the vine was a part of that blessing.

Dipping bread in vinegar (sometimes herbed vinegar), is still a prevalent custom of many cultures today. Suggesting that Ruth dip her bread into the common container of vinegar, shared by all, was to invite her into communion with them all. Boaz has already stated that she believes and trusts in the same God as they do and now he is inviting her to not only be one with them in belief but also one with them in community and the fellowship of a shared meal.

And She Sat Beside The Reapers:

Ruth has been careful of not being presumptuous. She now accepts the invitation of Boaz to join them all at table. She sits beside the reapers to share the meal. Boaz has shown everyone that he accepts her presence in their midst. He does this by his invitation and by implication he expects them to accept her also. At the invitation of Boaz, Ruth now has a place among the people of Naomi.

And He Reached Her Parched Corn,

Boaz is sitting with the reapers and sharing the meal with them. It is not beneath him to join them. He eats with them and talks with them; it is a time to relax, enjoy, and to take a break. Boaz has joined his laborers at table and has invited Ruth to join them too. She does and Boaz reaches out to Ruth to give her some of the cooked barley.

Barley that is in its natural state, that is not pearled, has a honey like, naturally sweet, nutty flavor. Parching it brings out even more of its delicious flavor; it is reminiscent, of roasted chestnuts. Barley is one of those rare near perfectly balanced foods giving the optimum proportion of protein, carbohydrates, and fat that the body needs. Boaz would have been hard put to offer her any food more perfect. His reaching out to her shows favor to her. We do not know what his motives are and perhaps he does not know them either but he does want to do something nice for her (even if on impulse) and he wants to please her. It is easy to see him smile at her as he reaches out to her and we can also easily see her smile in return as their eyes meet and she accepts his offer.

And She Did Eat,

Ruth is now sharing her first meal that is among the people of this land and of this particular locality in the land of Israel. Ruth's life and destiny is becoming tied to Bethlehem through shared experience. These are the ordinary people. These folk work hard for their living and these workers of the land, as a result, are in many ways the closest to it.

In early spring, as the soft velvet soil runs through their fingers, having been turned over and made ready for planting, it would be only natural to feel close to this ground that would bring forth, by the grace of God, an abundant crop. Many, many times, each one of them comes out to the field; first to see the tiny plants emerge and then to watch them grow day by day until one fine day it is harvest time. There is a solidarity that develops through shared work and the shared fruits of that labor. *And she did eat.*

And Was Sufficed,

Ruth had eaten and was satisfied. Her immediate need had been met. There is a comfort in being sufficed that reaches all the way into the soul. With comfort, there comes renewed strength, and a certain sense of security, and well being that reaches out towards the future. She ate *and was sufficed.*

And Left.

Ruth left the house as soon as she finished her meal, to resume her work. Gleaning was hard work for little gain but she meant to take advantage of every moment of daylight that she could. She was diligent and wasted no time in getting back to work.

She had much time to think. Gleaning occupied her physically but not mentally. There was time to ponder over all that had taken place on this first day in the field.

> *Ruth 2: 15 "And when she was risen up to glean, Boaz commanded his young men, saying, Let her glean even among the sheaves, and reproach her not:"*

And When She Was Risen Up To Glean,

Boaz has something to say to his reapers but he waits until Ruth has left. He is truly a gentleman and does not want to cause Ruth any embarrassment by talking about her in her presence. He also does not want to embarrass her in front of everyone by offering her open charity. When he sees that she has gone out of earshot and is once more gleaning, he speaks to all the young men.

Boaz Commanded His Young Men,

Boaz not only speaks to the young men, he lays down the law. There is to be no question or exceptions to what he is about to say. This is the way he wants it and this is the way it is going to be. The young men must clearly understand this. They listen carefully and will surely follow his instructions.

Let Her Glean Even Among The Sheaves,

It was a good thing that Boaz got their full attention and that everyone clearly understood what he was saying and what he wanted them to allow. This command was, while maybe not entirely unprecedented, at least highly unusual.

Boaz was telling the young men that it was all right for Ruth to collect grain among the sheaves that had already been harvested and bundled for him. Actually, Ruth had asked permission of the servant set over the reapers to glean among the sheaves. Since the sheaves were no doubt set up all over the harvested part of the field, the whole field was open territory. What may be in question is the grain directly around the bottom of the sheaves. No doubt, as the bundles or sheaves of grain were stood up, some would fall out around the sheaves. This was not technically overlooked grain in the field that was available to gleaners. It would be easy pickings for the gleaners to go close to the sheaves and pick up this loose grain that had accidentally fallen out of the sheaves and to the ground.

It seems that gleaners were usually told not to pick up

the grain that had fallen out of the sheaves. It could be that most farmers frowned upon gleaning this fallen grain. Perhaps they felt that surely this was not what the Lord had in mind when He allowed for gleaning. Why would anyone let the poor help themselves to that which had been already reaped and set-aside for the owner? After all, even if it had now dropped on the ground, it had been set-aside before it fell to the ground.

The point was probably arbitrary but Boaz was saying that Ruth could glean among the sheaves that had been set-aside for him. In this way (even though a small way) he was including her in his blessing and bounty.

And Reproach Her Not:

Boaz did not want them to chide Ruth at all. While the young men might have followed the letter of the law (as laid down by Boaz) they may not have followed the spirit of it. They could have allowed her to gather from among the sheaves but then have made rude or derogatory comments because of it. Boaz did not want Ruth to be put off by any negative attitude or words on the part of the young men. Boaz seeks to protect Ruth from any unpleasantness and therefore tells the young men not only to let her glean among the sheaves but they are also not to reproach her for it.

> *Ruth 2:16 "And let fall also some of the handfuls of purpose for her, and leave them, that she may glean them, and rebuke her not."*

And Let Fall Also Some Of The Handfuls Of Purpose For Her,

Boaz adds to what he has already said and voices something else that is also astonishing. He now tells the young men to allow some handfuls of barley to drop as if by accident. What can he be thinking? The young men must have wondered about this unorthodox charity. It would have been easier to simply give her some barley but Boaz has reasons for his method of providing for Ruth.

And Leave Them, That She May Glean Them,

Boaz is saying that Ruth is still going to have to work for what she gets. She is not just going to be handed charity. In doing this, he shows great wisdom, empathy, and insight along with a charitable spirit. He knows that Ruth, justifiably, feels that she has less than no claim to his kindness. She has pointed out to him that she is a persona non grata because of being a Moabite. In fact she has pointed this out to him twice. He also knows that she has dignity and, more to the point, is therefore willing to work hard for her sustenance. She asks only to be allowed to gather what would otherwise be left to rot in the field.

Boaz shows much sensitivity to her situation in life and comes up with this idea, which will protect her dignity and healthy self-respect. He decides, that if it seems an accident that the grain has been left behind, then Ruth will still have to work for it but he will have made her labors a little easier.

The young men understand what Boaz has said and even if they do not fully understand his motivation, they are willing to go along with what Boaz has requested. Actually, as we shall see, they entered into this charitable act quite enthusiastically.

And Rebuke Her Not.

Again, Boaz reiterates that the young men are not to rebuke Ruth. This time they are not to rebuke her for picking up the large and obvious handfuls that have been "accidentally" dropped. In stating this prohibition against rebuke a second time, he is hoping that the repetition will cause it to become fixed in their minds and that it will govern their actions and attitude.

His repeating the instructions as firm commands gives his words emphasis and more weight. He expects the young men to follow the letter of his law and they do to perhaps such an extent that it goes even beyond what Boaz had in mind. No doubt they enjoyed entering into this gracious form of charity because they were very generous with Boaz's bounty.

> *Ruth 2:17 "So she gleaned in the field until even, and beat out that she had gleaned: and it was about an ephah of barley."*

So She Gleaned In The Field

Ruth got up from the midday meal and went right back to work. It had been good to have a break and to have her hunger satisfied. Her heart was filled as well. She was truly refreshed. The afternoon stretched out with gentle sunlight across the field where she would search, inch by inch for hidden and forgotten grain.

There was no other world, no other life, and for her, no other reality. The hum of insects, the voices of the men and women, the earth below her feet, this was reality. This field had no part in the past. This field was her present and her future. *So she gleaned in the field.*

Until Even,

Ruth worked hard in the field, all afternoon, until dusk. It had been a very long hard day. She was more than tired. She was exhausted but happy with her results. The afternoon seemed to go better than had the morning. She had found more barley during the afternoon than she had in the morning. Perhaps the reapers were also tired and getting careless during the latter part of the long day.

She also felt a certain amount of contentment in her new life because someone had shown her kindness. No, a drink of water and a piece of bread are not big things but it was the kind spirit in which they were given which made all the difference. Yes she was tired, but wouldn't Naomi be surprised with her success at gleaning? It would be so good to see Naomi after this long hard day. It would soon be dark but first she had to beat out her grain.

And Beat Out That She Had Gleaned:

Ruth left the field to go to the threshing floor. Threshing floors were built nearby on a hill or rise in order to catch the breeze. During the daytime, for the most part, the air is still but towards evening the breeze picks up. This phenomenon is very helpful in the threshing process.

First the heads of grain must be broken off the stalk and then the head is beaten to loosen the grains from the head and to loosen husks from around the grain. This is done on the threshing floor. After beating, the grain was then tossed into the air and the wind would blow away the loosened and lighter chaff and husks but the grain being much heavier would fall back down to the floor where it could be scooped up. It was now ready for use. At dusk, when night was beginning to fall, Ruth completed this process with the stalks of grain she had gleaned.

And It Was About An Ephah Of Barley.

An ephah was about three pecks and three pints. A peck contains eight quarts or 8.8 liters. In other words, she has almost six and a half gallons of barley. That was an incredible amount of barley to have gleaned in one day.

When boiled, a cup of barley makes about four or so cups of delicious healthy food. This is perhaps enough for one day. What Ruth had gleaned in one day would feed her and Naomi for many, many days, actually about fifty days.

Part Six – Ruth Takes the Barley Home to Naomi Ruth 2:18 to Ruth 2:23

Ruth 2:18 "And she took it up, and went into the city and her mother-in-law saw what she had gleaned: and she brought forth, and gave to her that she had reserved after she was sufficed."

And She Took It Up,

Ruth gathered together all her grain and *she took it up*. The Hebrew word for *took it up* is nasa and it is a word packed with a wealth of meaning. Basically it means to lift up or to raise up. Nasa was used in chapter 1 and verse 4. *And they took them wives.* The same word was used in the story of Noah when the waters lifted up (nasa) the Ark. Concerning the forgiveness of sin, the scapegoat carried (nasa) away the sin of the people. Nasa also means to exalt or to extol. In addition, nasa is used to express the expectation that all will go well.

> "Yea the Almighty shall be thy defense, and thou shalt have plenty of silver. For then shalt thou have thy delight in the Almighty, and shalt lift up (nasa) thy face unto God. Thou shalt make thy prayer unto him, and he shall hear thee, and thou shalt pay thy vows."
> Job 22: 25-27

Ruth had put her trust in God and He was her defense and had indeed supplied her with plenty. She had to be delighted when she picked up (nasa) her huge amount of barley. Physically she may have been tired, aching, and totally exhausted but in her heart she had to be thrilled and delighted with the rewards of her hard work.

And Went Into The City

Ruth left the field behind as she carried her barley back to Bethlehem. Because she had so much, it would have weighed a considerable amount, about forty pounds. She *went into the city*, to the house where she and Naomi lived.

And Her Mother-In-Law Saw What She Had Gleaned:

It would have been priceless to see the look on Naomi's face when Ruth came in with all her barley. It was an amazing amount and for a moment Naomi was speechless.

And Gave To Her That She Had Reserved After She Was Sufficed.

We now learn that Ruth is not at all wasteful. She has saved what was left over from the parched barley that Boaz had given her in the house as she sat among the reapers to eat. He had told her to share the bread and to feel free to dip it in the vinegar along with everyone else. He had also given her more of the parched barley than she needed to satisfy her hunger and so she saved the rest for later. She takes it home with her along with all the barley she has gleaned. Ruth now gives Naomi the extra food that she had saved after she had had enough to eat.

> *Ruth 2:19 "And her mother-in-law said unto her, Where hast thou gleaned today? and where wroughtest thou? blessed be he that did take knowledge of thee. And she showed her mother-in-law with whom she had wrought, and said, The man's name with whom I wrought today is Boaz."*

And Her Mother-In-Law Said Unto Her.

It does not take Naomi long to find her voice. She may have been speechless for a slim moment when she saw the amount of barley that Ruth had brought home. She had not immediately said anything as Ruth handed her the food that she has gotten, from who knows where? But Naomi soon regains her ability to speak. She is going to ask some sharp questions and she expects some straight answers. She knows very well that this abundance that Ruth has come home with is not just a day's worth of gleaning. She knows that this amount is way out of the ordinary and she wants an explanation.

No one knows what may have been going through her mind or if she came to some preliminary conclusions of her own. We do know that she recovered her equilibrium quickly as was true to form for Naomi. She was taken aback but now she fires off one question and then another. She comments and she pronounces. We can see her standing there, hands on hips, but ready to believe anything Ruth may choose to tell her. Nevertheless, with no nonsense and like any mother would, Naomi wants some answers.

Were Hast Thou Gleaned Today?

In typical motherly fashion, Naomi asks, where have you been? When Ruth left home it was with hopes that someone would allow her to glean in his field. She was hoping to find enough grace in someone's eyes so she would be allowed to glean. Her desires were not grandiose. She did not pray that she would walk out and find a fortune waiting for her around the next bend in the road. All she wanted was a very small thing and that was to find the right person and the right situation where she would be allowed to work very hard for something that had been considered and was in reality of no account.

Was that too much to have asked? Was that being foolishly unrealistic? Was she indulging in unreasonable optimism? Hardly, and Naomi knew it. Naomi did not take the time for a long mental reasoning process. In her typically deft fashion of getting to the bottom line, so to speak, she knows that there is one question to ask which will begin to unravel the mystery of Ruth's bounty. *Where hast thou gleaned today?*

And Where Wroughtest Thou?

Naomi does not pause and give Ruth a chance to answer the question. Before Ruth can get in a word, Naomi fires off another question. *And where wroughtest thou?* The Hebrew word that has been translated wroughtest is asah. It basically means to work. Wrought is an old word for work and it is still used today as in wrought iron meaning iron that has been worked or shaped.

Naomi has used the word asah before, in her prayer for blessing for her daughters-in-law. In chapter one and verse eight we see it translated as deal. This is a good translation because included in the complete meaning of asah, is obeying and creating. Obeying the Lord is our work and His creation is His work.

Naomi had desired the Lord to deal (asah) kindly with her daughters-in-law as they had dealt (asah) kindly with her and those who had died. We see in the blessing of so much barley that God has heard Naomi's prayer and is pouring out blessing upon both of them through the kindness of Boaz.

Blessed Be He That Took Knowledge Of Thee.

Even before she gives Ruth a chance to answer the second questions, (let alone the first) Naomi's response to the yet unborn answer is keen and quick. She asks the Lord for a blessing on the person responsible for all the barley. She knows that Ruth did not come by all this barley through simply gleaning all day, in an unknown field, even though she had worked hard (and no doubt by the look of her, very hard.)

There had to be an explanation and Naomi is no fool. She appreciated the generosity of this unknown person and she is ready to call upon the Lord to bless the person, who is responsible, no matter who he is. She feels certain that someone has realized that they have desperate need and *took knowledge* of Ruth. That is to say, someone understood her situation and had taken pity on her. But who, who was their kind-hearted benefactor?

And She Showed Her Mother-In-Law With Whom She Had Wrought,

Ruth tells her mother-in-law about her tiring but exciting day. She relates in detail all that has happened. Ruth paints a vivid picture; she literally shows Naomi all that has happened. Ruth tells her about the owner coming from Bethlehem and blessing the reapers. She tells how they readily replied with a blessing for him. She tells how he spoke to her and her surprise that he should have taken notice of her.

Ruth goes on to tell Naomi how kind he had been in telling her that she was to stay close to his maidens and that he had told the young men not to take advantage of her just because she was different. Ruth then related that the man had said she was not even to think of going to glean in someone else's field, but to stay only in his fields and she was welcome to continue all during the whole barley harvest and even through the wheat harvest. After he said all this he invited her to share the meal with everyone and had even personally passed her more food than she could eat and that was why she had been able to bring some home for Naomi.

Ruth then told Naomi about how after the meal the gleaning had gone so well that she was able to bring home all this barley. It had been a good day.

And Said, The Man's Name With Whom I Wrought Today Is Boaz.

Almost as an afterthought and as if Naomi probably would not know very much, if anything, about this man, Ruth adds that the man in whose field she has been working is named Boaz. Beside the fact that Ruth did not know who Boaz was, we learn that he did not go back to Bethlehem after checking on the progress of the harvest, but rather had stayed to help. She says that she worked with him so he was out there working in the field also, which gave him plenty of time to observe Ruth and vice versa.

> *Ruth 2:20 "And Naomi said unto her daughter-in-law, Blessed be he of the LORD, who hath not left off his kindness to the living and to the dead. And Naomi said unto her, The man is near of kin unto us, one of our next kinsmen."*

And Naomi Said Unto Her Daughter-In-Law,

The relationship of family, which closely connects Naomi and Ruth is reemphasized over and over. Beyond and besides being two women who are staying together because they love each other, Naomi and Ruth are connected by marriage.

While it is true that the bond of love that binds them to each other is very strong, that is not what is being pointed out. What is being pointed out is their relationship as mother-in-law and daughter-in-law. When Ruth left home in the morning, she was Naomi's daughter. When she went out to glean, Naomi again called her daughter. Why then, after returning and showing what she has gleaned and after telling Naomi in whose field she has worked, does Naomi think of her again as a daughter-in-law? Naomi now speaks not to Ruth the person she loves as daughter, but *unto her daughter-in-law.*

Blessed Be He Of The Lord,

For a second time, Naomi calls upon the LORD to bless the man who has shown favor to Ruth. She truly wants him to be blessed and she knows that all blessing ultimately comes from God. Her trust in God to reward this person who has shown gracious generosity to them is uncomplicated and straightforward. She once again demonstrates her closeness to the Lord.

Her immediate reaction to what she has heard is directed to the Lord. Time and again she demonstrates the priority of her close relationship to Him by those immediate almost reflexive responses to call on Him. In speaking to Ruth, she first calls upon the Lord to bless this benefactor of theirs. She calls upon Him before she continues her conversation.

Who Hath Not Left Off His Kindness To The Living And To The Dead.

Naomi attributes all to God. She readily gives the glory to God. She again says that it is God who is responsible for the bounty that has come to them. She knows that it is God's hand behind the hand that has caused blessing to come into their lives. She and Ruth have trusted in the Lord and He has been faithful to them and provided graciously for them.

She says that God has not only shown kindness to them

but also to the dead. She may be thinking that, in the past, it had been their husbands' responsibility to provide for their wives. Now, since the death of their husbands, they have had to depend directly and solely upon the Lord to provide for them in place of their husbands. Since their husbands have failed in their duty (albeit they are dead) it is now left up to the Lord.

Since we have never seen Naomi waste any time in vain regret, it is not only possible but more than likely that she may not be thinking primarily of what had happened in the past and its repercussions for the present, but instead it is more likely that she is thinking of the present and of the future. Knowing Naomi and her eminent practicality, this is probably closer to the truth.

Naomi was a practical realist. She was not one to live in the past. She got on with life and was more than willing to give God a hand (it seems she just cannot help herself) as she had done in telling the young women to return to their homes in Moab so that their mothers could find them new husbands. She gives God all the glory though for His care of them, and does so readily in this instance.

The Hebrew word she uses for kindness is checed. It is a most important word because for Israel it had to do with God's covenant with Abraham and Isaac and Jacob and His loyalty and constant loving care. In a wider spectrum it has to do with all of mankind and creation (the Noah covenant was with all of mankind, the animals, and the earth.) It is not based on man's performance but rather it is a demonstrative part of God's unchanging nature to love. Checed is also tied to mercy and God's forgiveness of sin because of His eternal and unfailing love.

Naomi used this word before in her blessing for both her daughters-in-law. In chapter one and verse eight, Naomi had wanted the Lord to deal kindly with them in their future lives, just as they had dealt kindly with the dead and with her. Naomi is now saying that God has shown kindness to them. She actually says that here is proof that God is continuing to show them checed. It is something that is ongoing. He has not stopped showing them loving kindness.

And Naomi Said Unto Her,

This phrase is repeated from a few lines above. Naomi is still talking to Ruth but she is going to change the subject and make a new point. She had been talking about the Lord and how He has been looking after them. Now she is going to talk about a new subject.

This new subject has importance and is validated because Naomi, in effect, has just attributed what is happening in their lives (their being provided for) to God. She, in effect, has put the seal of God upon what she is going to say. In that respect one thought naturally flows out of the other and has natural continuity with the other. Naomi is about to make a revelation to Ruth. If Ruth had been astonished that this exalted man had taken notice of her, she will be even more astonished when she finds out who he is. She may have thought that his name would mean little if anything to Naomi, but this is far from the case.

The Man Is Near Of Kin Unto Us,

Naomi informs Ruth of their relationship to Boaz. Boaz is a close relative. This is obviously important to Naomi or she would not have mentioned it to Ruth. We wonder, as perhaps Ruth did, why Naomi had not told Ruth about their relative before this. Perhaps there were many relatives. Perhaps she had mentioned him before and with all the new faces and introductions, the mention of even more relatives was just too confusing. Perhaps Ruth just did not make the connection with all the new names and this man out in the field who had been kind to her.

At any rate, this announcement of his being related to them was news to Ruth. While interesting, it may have been less important to Ruth than to Naomi, as there are probably many relatives and friends of Naomi's that she has not yet met. Ruth may have looked a little blank or at least not as impressed as Naomi must have thought Ruth ought to be. Naomi tries to make the significance a little clearer. She spells it out for Ruth.

One Of Our Next Kinsmen.

In telling Ruth that Boaz is *one of our next kinsmen,* she is relating something very significant. This information that Boaz is a near kinsman was already related in chapter two verse one but this is apparently the first time that Ruth is being told about it.

As has been mentioned before, the actual Hebrew word for next kinsmen is goel (alternative spelling gaal.) It essentially means redeemer. According to the Mosaic Law, a brother or near relative could redeem, buy back, for a poor relative, a piece of land or animal etc. that he had had to sell.

> "If thy brother be waxen poor, and hath sold away some of his possession, and if any of his kin come to redeem it, then shall he redeem that which his brother sold. Leviticus 25:25

Another part of the goel law concerned a dead brother's childless widow. It was considered a duty to marry the widow and the first son of the union would inherit the dead man's name and estate. This kind of marriage was based on brotherly love, which was of great importance in Israelite society as the basis for morality. While a man was not bound by law to enter into marriage with his brother's widow, it was considered a reproach against him and his house if he refused. The widow then had the right to publicly humiliate him if he did not wish to marry her.

In telling Ruth that Boaz is *one of our near kinsmen,* she is telling her that Boaz is one of their relatives who could redeem their family land and marry her. The big question now is, would he be willing to do it. They know that he can afford to do so but what is the likelihood that this prominent citizen would want to marry a Moabitess?

> *Ruth 2:21 "And Ruth the Moabitess said, He said unto me also, Thou shalt keep fast by my young men, until they have ended all my harvest."*

And Ruth The Moabitess Said,

Ruth has not yet reached the point where Naomi's people have become her people in terms of national identity. She still, very much, thinks of herself as a Moabitess. She is very much aware that what Naomi might be suggesting as a possibility, in all reality may be hampered by her origins. When she answers Naomi it is not just Ruth the beloved daughter but also as *Ruth the Moabitess.*

He Said Unto Me Also,

Ruth responds to what Naomi has explained, with

information that she feels will give Naomi reason to believe that Boaz is not completely indifferent to her. It is interesting that Ruth does not demur for an instant concerning the not so subtle suggestion that Naomi has raised. Ruth clearly shows her willingness to the idea of marrying Boaz by her wanting to give Naomi even the slenderest evidence that Boaz may not be completely indifferent to her. Could it be, was it possible that Ruth had felt a strong attraction to Boaz on their very first meeting? How romantic.

There seems to be evidence against this idea in that Ruth did not stay in the house after she had finished eating but instead immediately left to go back to her gleaning. If she did feel an attraction, why did she not linger, with the hopes of further conversation?

Perhaps, she realized the impossibility of their ever being together. Her mother-in-law had warned her of the lonely life that awaited her in Bethlehem if she insisted on coming with her. If she wanted to marry and have a happy home with a husband and children, she should have gone back to Moab when she had the chance. No one in Israel would want to marry her, let alone this attractive, wealthy, prominent leader in the community.

Ruth knew she had to leave the house where Boaz was. It was better to just work and not to indulge in idle fancy. Naomi would surely have told her that. No one must know of her feelings and especially not Boaz. And yet, her feelings are so easily betrayed in her ready answer to Naomi.

Thou Shalt Keep Fast By My Young Men,

Ruth readily adds to what she has already told Naomi. She tells Naomi that beyond all Boaz has already said, he also told her that she should stay close to the young men who are doing all the reaping and bringing in the harvest. It would seem that Boaz trusts the young men to maintain proper respect and also to protect her along with all his maidens that are helping with the harvest. This shows helpful concern for Ruth and at least a passing interest in her welfare.

Until They Have Ended All My Harvest.

Boaz has suggested that Ruth stick with his harvesters through the harvest of all his different crops. This will give her the freedom to glean in his fields until the autumn season. Ruth will be sure of a friendly welcome and the lack of harassment that she might find in other fields. Ruth, by sharing all this with Naomi, indicates that she feels that Boaz has not only spoken to her in admiration but has certainly shown her special favor.

> *Ruth 2:22 "And Naomi said unto Ruth her daughter-in-law, it is good, my daughter, that thou go out with his maidens, that they meet thee not in any other field."*

And Naomi Said Unto Ruth Her Daughter-In-Law,

Interestingly, Ruth has once again become Ruth, Naomi's daughter-in-law and not Ruth the Moabitess (see previous verse.) This is because her relationship to Naomi is what is important in the context of being married to a kinsman redeemer. Naomi is not entirely clear as to how this could all work out and has to give the subject some thought.

She has definitely maintained her authoritative role in this little fragment of a family and she considers what is best to be done for the present. The idea of Boaz as Ruth's kinsman redeemer is new and Naomi realizes that there is no overt indication that Boaz has acted in any way more than as a kindly person would to a poor young widow. It is true that it seems that he has really gone far out of his way to be helpful but it will not do any good to refine too much on that.

It must be acknowledged that it has been ten years since she has seen him and she really cannot assume that she knows him very well after all this time. It will be well to proceed cautiously and step carefully for a while until she can see her way clearly.

It Is Good, My Daughter That Thou Go Out With His Maidens,

Naomi considers and concludes that for the present, Ruth should continue gleaning with Boaz's maidens. It is good for Ruth to be in a somewhat protected environment. All of Boaz's staff have been respectful of Ruth and know that Boaz has taken at least a cursory interest in her plight.

While working in Boaz's fields she would, more than likely, be seen by him again. She is a sweet, modest, beautiful girl. Who knows what kind of a fancy a man might take? At least, this way, Boaz will see Ruth, probably every day. She also seemed to find plenty of grain while gleaning in his field. All around, there were advantages to her walking out of Bethlehem in the company of his maidens and staying near them and the young men while out working in the fields.

That They Meet Thee Not In Any Other Field.

Naomi continues to consider what would be best for Ruth to do and comes up with another reason for Ruth to continue in the harvest fields of Boaz. She says that it would not look good for the maidens helping with the harvest to see her elsewhere. It would be better *that they meet thee not in any other field*

There were several possible reasons for why it would be better for Ruth not to be seen by the maidens of Boaz, in another field. The maidens might take offense, thinking that she did not want to work with them. Boaz had publicly told Ruth to stay with the maidens. Worse yet, Boaz might take offense if she did not listen to him and she would no longer have the protection that his interest in her engendered. She also might not be seen by him on a daily basis, a sort of out of sight, out of mind situation. Naomi definitely thought that it would be better for Ruth to stay with the maidens of Boaz and not be seen in another field.

This word field (sadeh) has now been used fourteen times. Seven times were in reference to the fields (country or countryside) of Moab and seven others were in reference to the fields of Bethlehem. The balance will be tilted to the side of promise with the last two uses.

> *Ruth 2:23 "So she kept fast by the maidens of Boaz to glean unto the end of barley harvest and of wheat harvest; and dwelt with her mother-in-law."*

So She Kept Fast By The Maidens Of Boaz

Ruth did as Boaz and Naomi had said she should do and stayed in the vicinity of where the maidens were working to help with the harvest. She worked hard and continued gleaning. It is likely that the young men continued to drop extra handfuls of grain, here and there, so that she was "helped" in her efforts but it was still hard, back-breaking, work.

To Glean Unto The End Of Barley Harvest And Of Wheat Harvest;

There is a consistency in what Ruth does. She makes up her mind and sees a thing through without complaint or any hint of resentment about the hard work or her lot in life. Ruth continued to go out every day until the end of the barley and wheat harvest.

In the harvesting of barley there is a two-week period of optimum time as to when the barley should be harvested. Before this two-week period, the grain is not totally mature and contains too much moisture making it susceptible to rotting in storage. There are hopes and prayers that the weather will be fair and dry so that the harvest can proceed. The grain must be dry and there is time needed to get the laborious work done and it is all done by hand. After the two-week period, the grain heads are susceptible to disease such as smut and the seed heads start to open and drop the precious grain to the ground.

So, Ruth continued to glean to the end of the barley harvest. The wheat harvest follows hard on the heels of the barley harvest as it ripens just two weeks later. It also has this two-week period of optimum time to harvest. Ruth worked through the wheat harvest also, staying with the maidens and young men who were working for Boaz. It is more than likely that Ruth saw Boaz on a daily basis and he saw her.

And Dwelt With Her Mother-In-Law.

Ruth continues to work to support her mother-in-law

and herself. She returns each evening with the grain she has worked so hard to glean. They dwell together in a loving relationship and even though Ruth is the material supporter of this family, Naomi is still the head of the household and Ruth respects Naomi and acknowledges her position in this family. Naomi has not become a dependant of Ruth due to material dependence. What was important was not where the next dime came from (so to speak) or even where all the dimes came from but that their relationship remained the same.

In our day, when money rules, money is power, and money has the last word and sometimes the only word. This modern viewpoint makes it hard to understand the relationship of authority and subordination that existed between Naomi and Ruth. If Naomi and Ruth had lived in a culture that placed major importance on the material, then, an individual's role and significance in life would be based on having "the goods". If the values and priorities of this day had been the same in those days, it would have soon been Naomi that was dwelling with Ruth.

This never happened because Ruth and Naomi were not looking at life through materialistic eyeglasses. Their premise for the way they viewed and lived life was based on their paradigm belief in God. They knew that God ordered all the events in their lives, including their positions. And they knew that they could safely place their trust in Him.

Living in this belief system, not only gave their life meaning, it also helped to define it. It provided for them a rock solid stability. God loved them and cared for them. Their lives were governed not only by His immutable laws but also by their knowledge of His character. Since position in life is not based on money or goods in any amount (and neither is it based on a lack of them), then who brought the money (or grain) into their home did not matter in determining roles in life. What did give their lives significance was both their relationship with God and with each other and to the community around them. This relationship is emphasized by the fact that we are told not that Ruth continued to dwell with Naomi but that she *dwelt with her mother-in-law.*

Chapter Three

Part Seven –
Naomi Decides on a Husband for Ruth and Instructs Her
Ruth 3:1 to Ruth 3:6

Ruth 3:1 "Then Naomi her mother-in-law said unto her, My daughter, shall I not seek rest for thee, that it may be well with thee?"

Then Naomi Her Mother-In-Law Said Unto Her,

Naomi has never stopped being concerned for Ruth. Ruth has come home at the end of the day and relates all that has happened. Naomi turns over in her mind what the future holds for her lovely loving Ruth. She had warned

Ruth even before they got to Bethlehem, that her future at best would be grim. She had told her that hope for a husband and children and to be happily married in a home of her own, was only possible in Moab. Yes, she had really tried so hard to make her see reason but Ruth stubbornly would not even consider it. She had clung to her with such unbendable resolution. There had been no changing her steadfast decision, so Naomi had had to give it up.

Since they had arrived in Bethlehem, Naomi had much time to consider what would be best for her dear Ruth. Maybe, just maybe, there was a possible glimmer of hope. She decides that since she is Ruth's mother-in-law she needs to talk to Ruth. She decides to approach the whole question of Ruth's future from a reasoned and reasonable viewpoint.

My Daughter,

Naomi chooses to speak to Ruth from a position stronger than the social and legal position that she has as Ruth's mother-in-law. She begins what she has to say by calling Ruth *my daughter*. Naomi could not love Ruth any more than if she were indeed a daughter. This love that she has for Ruth is the pure motivation for what she is about to say to Ruth. Naomi is speaking out of love.

Shall I Not Seek Rest For Thee,

In essence, what Naomi is saying is that she thinks she ought to find a husband for Ruth. The idea of Naomi arranging a match for Ruth was not an unusual arrangement. For the most part, parents were the ones who arranged marriages for their children. Naomi, therefore, bases her proposition to find a husband for Ruth on her logical recognition of her responsibility to Ruth. As Ruth's mother, it would be her responsibility to find a husband for Ruth.

What, of course, must have been surprising to Ruth was the whole idea of a marriage being possible after Naomi had vehemently assured her that, if she persisted in coming to Bethlehem, she would have no chance for a husband, family, and home. Now Naomi is saying that she thinks she ought to go out and see what she can do for Ruth in order to *seek rest for thee.*

The use of the word rest has been discussed before (chapter 1, verse 9.) It includes more than just marriage. It speaks of finding a settled place in life, which quite naturally included a husband, children, and a happy home life with all the joys, pleasures and responsibilities that would include. As has been said, women were free to have businesses and other pursuits in life but true happiness and fulfillment in life was all about relationship and the opportunity for the closest relationship was found in the bonds of marriage.

That It May Be Well With Thee?

Naomi appreciates the loving care that Ruth has shown towards her and she loves her dearly. Ruth means all the world to her and because of her unselfish love for Ruth she wants a full life for Ruth. She knows that Ruth will not have a full and fulfilling life if she continues alone with her. She asks Ruth, should not I find a husband *that it may be well with thee?*

The Hebrew word for *well* is yatab and basically means good, lovely, pleasant, and beautiful. Another example of the use of this word, yatab is found in Genesis when Jacob the son of Isaac is reminding God of His promise.

> "And Jacob said, O God of my father

> Abraham, and God of my father Isaac, the LORD which saidst unto me, Return unto thy country, and to thy kindred, and I will deal well (yatab) with thee:" Genesis 32: 9

God had entered into a covenant relationship with the patriarchs and people of Israel and as part of the covenant God had promised to bless them. Naomi wanted Ruth to have this same kind of yatab in the covenant of marriage.

> *Ruth 3:2 "And now is not Boaz of our kindred, with whose maidens thou wast? Behold, he winnoweth barley tonight in the threshingfloor."*

And Now Is Not Boaz Of Our Kindred,

Naomi forthrightly gives Ruth the one reason why Boaz should marry her. There is no hesitation or vagary or coy dissimulation about her presentation of this fact to Ruth. It is their one and only claim upon him. Naomi's argument goes as straight as an arrow to the heart of the matter. She has decided that Boaz is Ruth's one best chance for marriage. It is in no way a sure thing that Boaz will be willing to marry Ruth. Boaz cannot be forced to marry her and Naomi knows this.

Ruth could not forget Naomi's strong assertion that there was no hope for her in Israel and yet here is Naomi suggesting that there is a chance. What has made Naomi change her mind? She has always known that she has kinsmen here in Bethlehem. Why then has she come to the conclusion that one of them might be willing to marry her and why this particular kinsman/redeemer? Why Boaz?

Is it because he is rich? Are not there others in the family who could also fulfill this role? Has Naomi gotten some hint that Boaz is not completely indifferent to Ruth? What are the small, almost insignificant things that Ruth has related to Naomi about her days in the field that might cause Naomi to start thinking along these lines? What has Naomi heard in the town of Bethlehem among the people?

All it would take is an unguarded look by Boaz in Ruth's direction to start some of the gossips. Had not the young men come in from the field with reports of the efforts of Boaz on behalf of Ruth? What was a friendly gossip to make of that? There was much room for speculation with a mysterious exotic Moabite flavor stirred in. Surely Naomi had heard some sly innuendoes and had been asked some artfully arch questions. And again, Naomi was no one's fool. She knew there had to be some basis for Boaz's unusual kindness. She was willing to take a chance that there was at least a little more than pure altruism behind his actions.

Never one to loose an opportunity, Naomi has made her typically quick decision and is ready to take a risk even in the face of failure. Hesitation is not her middle name. Although Ruth may be somewhat used to Naomi's sudden starts, she must have wondered what was coming next.

With Whose Maidens Thou Wast?

Ruth may well wonder why the question. Yes, she had been gleaning and staying close to the maidens of Boaz. What is the point? Obviously this is an important part of Naomi's logical reasoning, but how does it fit?

Naomi is using Ruth's experience to explain her logic. Of all their kinsmen, (and we have no idea how many there are) this particular kinsman is the one that Naomi feels Ruth should marry. She points out that this is the man, with whose maidens Ruth has been. In a way, Naomi is pointing out that Ruth already has an in. Not only is this the man who has shown surprising kindness to her, but also he knows, at least to a certain extent that he can trust her character. This is because she has been known to his maidens all this time and thus to a certain extent has also been known, through them to Boaz.

Behold,

Again we have the word *behold.* It is a word that says, sit up, pay attention and take note of what I am about to say. Naomi knew that Ruth's whole future could hang in the balance with what was about to take place. What was said and done this night could irrevocably decide the future. Naomi is very aware that Ruth must understand this. Naomi is about to give Ruth specific instructions as to what she should do. Naomi is saying to Ruth that what she is about to say is very important and Ruth should take careful note.

He Winnoweth Barley Tonight In The Threshingfloor.

Somehow, Naomi has heard that Boaz will be winnowing his barley tonight. It has been a couple of weeks since the end of the barley harvest and it is time to prepare the grain for use and then put it in storage.

As has been mentioned, a breeze comes up in the evening making this the best time to winnow. As Ruth had done, (chapter 2, verse 16) the grain heads are first flailed or beaten to loosen the grain. Then the grain is tossed into the air so that the wind will blow away the chaff. The grain then falls down again onto the threshing floor.

Grain in any sizable amount is heavy and depending on

the amount, this process can be long hard work. There are many places in the world today that still use this same manual way of separating the grain from the chaff. The whole process is called winnowing.

After winnowing, the grain can then be scooped up for storage to be used throughout the year until the next harvest in the following spring. Naomi is telling Ruth that she has heard that tonight is the night that Boaz and those helping him will be at the threshing floor to do the winnowing of his barley.

> *Ruth 3:3 "Wash thyself therefore, and anoint thee, and put thy raiment upon thee, and get thee down to the floor: but make not thyself known unto the man, until he shall have done eating and drinking."*

Wash Thyself Therefore, And Anoint Thee, And Put Thy Raiment Upon Thee,

Naomi now tells Ruth that there are certain steps Ruth must take in order to facilitate her plan to find a husband for Ruth; the husband she has in mind being Boaz. She has told Ruth that Boaz is the man for her, the one she should marry. Now Naomi is telling Ruth how this is to be accomplished.

She gives her instructions. Step one is to take a bath. Again, we see the very practical side of Naomi. While the aphorism cleanliness is next to godliness may not be found in the Scriptures, it was a cardinal rule for a young lady who wants to interest a gentleman (or vice-versa) even back then. Naomi, leaving nothing (not even the obvious) to chance, tells Ruth to *wash thyself*.

Next she tells Ruth to anoint herself. Beauty aids even a few thousand years ago included oils and perfume. Naomi tells Ruth that now, as perhaps never before, is the time to use them.

A final step is to get dressed up. Perhaps, until now, Ruth has been wearing the clothes of a widow. Naomi is saying that the time has come for Ruth to get dressed up and look her best. This will also help Boaz to see her not as another man's widow but rather as an attractive eligible young lady.

And Get Thee Down To The Floor:

Naomi gives Ruth further instructions. After Ruth has done all that Naomi instructs her to do in preparing to appear her best, Naomi tells her she is to go down to the threshing floor where everyone has been working. This is where Boaz will be. Ruth must have wondered what was coming next in the way of directions from Naomi. Naomi continued.

But Make Not Thyself Known Unto The Man,

Naomi tells Ruth not to let Boaz see her. She is to stay out of his line of vision and not to draw attention to herself. He is not to see her in her festive clothes. (The clothes of a widow would have probably identified her immediately.) He is not to even know that she is there.

Until He Shall Have Done Eating And Drinking.

Naomi may have been working under the assumption that it is not a good policy to ask anything of a hungry and tired man. She knows that Boaz will be more likely to be receptive to her plan when he has had time to relax and enjoy a meal. He will feel the satisfaction of hard work well done and the knowledge that the crop has been harvested and made ready for the needs of the coming year. The relief of having finished the job, and a good celebration meal, will go a long way towards putting him in a receptive mood.

Naomi also tells Ruth that she is not to let Boaz see her even after all the work is done and everyone is happily relaxing over a well-deserved meal. She is not to let him see her even after he has finished eating and drinking. By this time he will be sleepy, his hunger will be satisfied, and he will be happily relieved that the work is all but done. The bountiful harvest will be ready for taking into Bethlehem so that he and his household will have plenty to last them during the coming year. The first crop of the year will have been secured and that would have to lend a great feeling of contented satisfaction.

> *Ruth 3:4 "And it shall be, when he lieth down, that thou shalt mark the place where he shall lie, and thou shalt go in, and uncover his feet, and lay thee down; and he will tell thee what thou shalt do."*

And It Shall Be, When He Lieth Down, That Thou Shalt Mark The Place Where He Shall Lie,

After the washing and anointing and going down to the threshing floor, there are just a couple of more steps in Naomi's instructions. She tells Ruth that she is to watch and make note of where Boaz is going to lie down and sleep for the night. The grain cannot be left there for anyone to help himself, so the workers sleep on the threshing floor near the fruits of their hard labor. Night will have fallen and there may be light from the moon enough to see dimly and at any rate, to the best of her ability, Ruth is to make a note of where Boaz is going to sleep.

And thou Shalt Go in, And Uncover His Feet,

Feet are a very significant part of the body. While they are the most distant part of the body from the head where all decisions are made in a person's life, the feet have to be relied on to take one to his desired destination.

Today we have an expression that says put feet to your words meaning, talk is not enough; action is also needed. Ruth was to uncover Boaz's feet so that his feet would be exposed.

Although it was the actual physical feet of Boaz that Naomi wanted Ruth to uncover, Naomi was also telling Ruth to uncover in a symbolic way what his actions will be towards her. She is telling Ruth to find out what Boaz's reactions may be to the idea of marrying her.

And Lay Thee Down;

Ruth had once before prostrated herself at the feet of Boaz. Naomi is telling Ruth that she is to lay herself down again at his feet, a very submissive position. Naomi has told Ruth that she is to present herself very attractively pure on the outside. This will emphasize physically what cannot be seen and that is her virtuous heart and spiritual life.

And He Will Tell Thee What Thou Shalt Do.

By following Naomi's instructions, it is possible that the rest of Ruth's future life will be decided on this very night. The thought must have been totally, or at the very least, a bit overwhelming. Will Boaz be willing to marry her? It is now time for Ruth to decide if she will follow Naomi's plan or not. Does she really want to marry Boaz? Naomi is sure that Boaz will decide in favor of marrying Ruth. She already sees Boaz setting forth plans and telling Ruth what she should do next.

In Hebrew, the word for do is asah. We have seen this word before. Naomi used it in her blessing for her daughters-in-law. She wanted the Lord to deal (asah) kindly with Orpah and Ruth because they had dealt (asah) kindly with those who had died and with her. Later Ruth asks Boaz why he has been so kind to her and he says it is because he has been told how she has dealt (asah) with her mother-in-law.

Asah has a broader meaning than to deal or to do. It has in its meaning the ideas to build, to construct, to create, to accomplish, to prepare, to handle and to be done. Naomi is saying that Boaz will know what to do next and will tell Ruth what she must do.

It is time for Ruth to decide. What will she do? In Naomi's mind there is no question. Once again, Naomi has made up her mind and decides on immediate action. She has prayed much and she knows that this is the course that Ruth should take and this is the exact moment to take it.

Naomi also knows that Boaz will not only decide whether to marry Ruth but will tell her what their next step should be. In this sense of asah, Boaz will build, construct, create and accomplish a plan. Naomi is convinced that Ruth need only to follow all her instructions and a beautiful "happily ever after" awaits her.

Will Ruth follow through with Naomi's plan even

though she may have doubts about such an exalted person wanting her for his wife? Will her courage fail her on the way to the threshing floor?

> *Ruth 3:5 "And she said unto her, All that thou sayest unto me I will do."*

And She Said Unto Her,

Ruth's response to Naomi is immediate. She does not hesitate to give herself time to form her answer in terms that will be acceptable to her mother-in-law. She does not need to.

All That Thou Sayest Unto Me I Will Do.

Ruth's response to Naomi is to tell her that she will do everything that Naomi has told her to do. She will unquestioningly obey. She totally trusts Naomi and is willing to trust her judgment as the person who is in authority over her and perhaps that is made easier because she knows that Naomi loves her and has her best interests at heart. In submitting to Naomi's authority to tell her what she should do, she is actually freeing herself to surrender to God's plan for her life.

Once before, Naomi had insisted that Ruth take a life changing action for her own benefit and Ruth refused. Why then is one time refusing to obey authority a part of God's plan and this time obeying is also a part of God's plan? And how could Ruth tell the difference?

In the first instance, Ruth refused to go back to Moab even though Naomi pleaded and threatened dire circumstances if Ruth insisted on not obeying Naomi's command to go back to Moab. Now here in this second major decision, Ruth decides to obey and go to the threshing floor. To obey and not to obey, how could both be right?

The answer is not that Naomi's authority is only marginal and in reality of little importance. This is not the case. Naomi had real authority. What made the difference were the consequences of obedience. Ruth and Naomi had a very close and loving relationship. If Ruth had decided (obedience is always a decision) to go back to Moab it would have broken her relationship with Naomi. Ruth had also come to trust and love the God of Israel. If she had decided to go back it would probably have meant breaking her relationship with God. She could neither break her relationship with God nor Naomi so she had to disobey.

In obeying Naomi to get ready and go down to the threshing floor, Ruth would not be breaking her relationship with God or Naomi and that is what made the difference.

> *Ruth 3: 6 "And she went down to the floor, and did according to all that her mother-in-law bade her."*

And She Went Down To The Floor,

Ruth puts feet to what she has said she would do and gets herself ready. She then goes down to the threshing floor. One wonders how difficult this was for Ruth knowing that with every step that when she talked to Boaz she could easily be rebuffed. Or, on the other hand, and perhaps even more disconcerting, Boaz might agree to Naomi's plan for them to marry. Marriage was a very big step and how well did she know Boaz? She was not indifferent to him. He had been very kind and understanding. Was it enough to trust her heart?

And Did According To All That Her Mother-In-Law Had Bade Her.

Ruth follows Naomi's instructions to the letter. She bathed, she put on perfume, and she put on her best clothes, and goes down to the threshing floor. She then mingled with everyone being sure to stay out of the sight of Boaz. After the dinner she noted where on the floor he decided to bed down. While many of the workers would stay also, it is probable that they kept their distance out of respect and in effect leaving him somewhat alone. Ruth made note of the spot where he was going to sleep and then probably took a place with the other maidens to wait until everyone was asleep.

Part Eight – Ruth Asks Boaz to Marry Her and He Answers Her Ruth 3:7 to Ruth 3:15

Ruth 3:7 "And when Boaz had eaten and drunk, and his heart was merry, he went to lie down at the end of the heap of corn: and she came softly, and uncovered his feet, and laid her down."

And When Boaz Had Eaten And Drunk And His Heart Was Merry,

Boaz was in the best possible mood. His crop was harvested and it had been a good one. He had eaten and had drunk and he was very satisfied and happy to the point of being merry. Life was good and God had been good to him.

Naomi had been right. If there was ever going to be a propitious moment, it was now.

He Went To Lie Down At The End Of The Heap Of Corn:

Boaz is tired. It is time for some much deserved and needed rest. Winnowing has been hard work but they have a huge heap of barley to show for all their work. There will be plenty for the next whole year. As mentioned before (see chapter two, verse two) corn is the older generic name for grain.

Boaz goes to one end of the huge heap. This will afford him some measure of privacy in his sleep as the rest of the laborers go to the other end and lower sides to sleep.

And She Went Softly,

Still following the instructions of Naomi, Ruth waits until everyone is asleep and then she gets up. It probably did not take long for everyone to fall asleep since everyone was tired and comfortably filled with food and drink. She very quietly moves to where Boaz is sleeping. No one sees her; no one hears her.

And Uncovered His Feet And Laid Herself Down.

Just as Naomi had told her to do, Ruth gently uncovers the bare feet of Boaz. She then snuggles down horizontally to him and waits. She has not awakened him. No one can have expected her to sleep. She waits for something to happen and perhaps thinks of how very far she has come since her tender years in Moab. On this night, Moab was a world away.

Ruth 3:8 "And it came to pass at

midnight, that the man was afraid, and turned himself: and, behold, a woman lay at his feet."

And It Came To Pass At Midnight,

The phrase, *and it came to pass* takes us back to the very first verse of the book of Ruth. All of history had moved forward toward these people (Elimelech and each individual in this story.) They lived at this place (Bethlehem), at this time (during the time of the judges.) Then because of a time of famine in the land, Elimelech and his family moved to Moab.

The second *and it came to pass* occurred when Naomi and Ruth arrived in Bethlehem. The entire city was moved about them. Everyone was astonished because of what had happened to this family and felt incredulous that such a family could suffer such severe reverses. Disaster was what had come to pass in their lives.

And now we have a third *it came to pass,* three being the number of God. The light of the new day had not yet dawned but it was here. It had already begun; it was midnight.

That The Man Was Afraid, And Turned Himself:

Boaz was severely startled. The Hebrew word that has been translated as afraid is charad. Its primary meaning is shaking such as the earth shaking in an earthquake. It can mean trembling with fear or simply startled. Ruth gave him a severe start and he turned himself over to see what had caused him to wake up.

And, Behold, A Woman Lay At His Feet.

To his great surprise there was a woman at his feet. Probably feeling something warm by his feet had caused him to wake up and his first thought probably was that it was some kind of animal. It is not uncommon in poor third-world countries today to have a rat snuggle in bed with a sleeping person. They come in search of warmth on a cool night. To find out that it was a woman down by his feet astounded him.

> *Ruth 3:9 "And he said, Who art thou? And she answered, I am Ruth thine handmaid: spread therefore thy skirt over thine handmaid; for thou art a near kinsman."*

And He Said, Who Art Thou?

Boaz's natural reaction is that he wants to know who she is. It is again obvious that he has not expected to find a woman in his makeshift bed, not even at the bottom of it. He is an honorable man and has not been involved in sin with a woman. He has a position of respect in the community and the law was very clear and drastic concerning that kind of sin. He innocently has no idea who this woman can be. Therefore, the first question out of his mouth is *who art thou?* There is no thought of taking advantage of the situation. All he wants to know, and immediately, is who she is before he asks the next obvious questions, "What are you doing here?" and. "What do you want?".

And She Answered,

Her answer comes as quickly as his question came. She is not here for a dalliance. She is here for one reason only. She wants to present her own question and she wants him to give her an answer, yea or nay.

I Am Ruth Thine Handmaid:

Ruth wastes no time in telling Boaz who she is. It is interesting and in light of what she is going to propose, significant, that she does not say that she is Ruth, the widow of Mahlon, thereby stressing their relationship. She tells him that she is Ruth and she adds that she is his handmaid. She is not his handmaid because she has worked for him. She has not. She says that she is his handmaiden simply as a social form of address indicating that she acknowledges that his position in society is far higher than her lowly position.

Spread Therefore Thy Skirt Over Thine Handmaid;

Ruth does not allow Boaz the time to ask her the why question. Why is she here? If she had, it would have put her in the position of having to defend and justify herself. Perhaps she did not even consciously realize that but in any case she moves on quickly continuing to talk and tells him why she is here.

There is another reason for her hasty revelation as to why she is here. She does not want him to come to any wrong conclusions. She is not here for a sexual encounter. She immediately asks him to marry her. The expression she uses is *spread therefore thy skirt over thine handmaid.* It is an idiomatic expression that leaves no room for doubt as to its meaning. She is seeking marriage.

The Hebrew word for skirt is kanap and means the bottom half of a robe. A robe is much fuller at the bottom than it is at the shoulders and therefore came to mean the fullest possibility for a relationship, which is marriage.

Whether or not he recalls it, in his blessing for her, back in their first encounter out in the field, Boaz had said that Ruth had come to trust in the Lord and come under His wings. The wings are the widest part of a bird. It is also a place of safety, security, rest, and comfort, next to the mother's heart and soft downy breast. Ruth has used the same Hebrew word (kanap) for marriage as Boaz used for wings. They are the same word.

This imagery is again poetic. Ruth's request is to trust in the outstretched robe of Boaz (marriage). Naomi's plan has been daring and Ruth's carrying it out is audaciously courageous. How dare she propose a marriage between Boaz and herself? What can justify her actions and request?

For Thou Art A Near Kinsman.

Ruth now gives her justification for her request. Naomi has already made it clear to Ruth that it is not a priority with her to have an heir for the family. She has never once mentioned it. She is interested in finding "rest" for Ruth. Her love for Ruth causes her to be deeply concerned for Ruth's future and above all she wants to see her settled in life. Ruth's future has been much on her mind but until now, she had seen no hope for Ruth.

Now Naomi feels that perhaps since Boaz has shown himself concerned and not entirely indifferent to Ruth, that there is a possibility he may decide to marry Ruth especially if he is given a logical reason as to why he should do so. The fact that he is a near kinsman, or goel (redeemer), would justify the marriage not only for him but also in the eyes of the whole community. She gives him that reason in saying *for thou art a near kinsman.* Ruth stops here. She must have held her breath as she awaited his answer.

> *Ruth 3:10 "And he said, Blessed be thou of the LORD, my daughter: for thou hast shown more kindness in the latter end than in the beginning, inasmuch as thou followedst not young men, whether poor or rich."*

And He Said, Blessed Be Thou Of The Lord,

How strange his reaction seems after all that Ruth has done and now said. There is surely bemusement in his voice and words. His reaction shows that he sees her as one standing on a high and holy pedestal. Her character is above reproach and he again, as he had done on that day in the field, wishes for her to be blessed by the Lord.

Boaz has been startled out of sleep and shocked to find a woman at the foot of his bed. And then finding out that it is Ruth, his reaction is to utter the same sentiment that he had desired for her on the first day he saw her in the field.

He had said before on their first meeting, *The LORD recompense thy work, and a full reward be given thee of the LORD God of Israel, under whose wings thou art come to trust.* This time he echoes what he has said in *blessed be thou of the Lord* as if nothing at all unusual has occurred in the middle of this night.

Whether he is still groggy from sleep or is now wide-awake makes no difference. His first reaction to the presence of Ruth is to bring God into this precious moment to sanctify it with the blessing of the Lord.

My Daughter,

Boaz again calls Ruth his daughter as he had done on the first day he talked to her. It is again an expression of how he sees his social position and responsibility in that position. Boaz takes being a responsible person very seriously and his sense of responsibility may help to sway his decision concerning his marrying Ruth.

For Thou Hast Shown More Kindness In The Latter End Than At The Beginning.

Boaz still does not answer her request. He analyzes what Ruth has done. He deals first on the spiritual plane and tells her that in coming to him she has demonstrated even more kindness towards Naomi than before. Can he have figured out that it is really Naomi who is behind this proposal? If so he does not mention it. Rather, he dwells on Ruth and gives her credit for showing kindness in this action whether it was her idea or not.

He does not feel that she has any selfish motives. He feels that he must honor her for being willing to marry him in order to benefit her mother-in-law. He said before that he had heard all about how she had dealt kindly with Naomi after the death of their husbands. He has seen how hard she has worked, day after day in order to support them both and now she is willing to sacrifice her entire future and become his wife. Her kindness to Naomi does not become weary over the hard times; it only grows and that is something that Boaz recognizes as very rare and sacrificial on the altar of love.

Inasmuch As Thou Followedst Not Young Men, Whether Poor Or Rich.

Inasmuch is a word that connects a conclusion to the presentation of the facts. Boaz has already as good as told Ruth that he believes she has come with her proposal with unselfish motives. He believes that she is doing this for Naomi's benefit. He has stated that in wishing to marry him she is showing supreme kindness; even more than before.

The proof for him is that she has *followedst not young men.* In the opinion of Boaz, Ruth is a beautiful young woman who is naturally attractive to young men. He says that it is known that she has not sought the company of any of the young men in Bethlehem. Boaz must have been keeping track of Ruth or at least had been listening to the speculation about her in order to have this information.

He knows she has not encouraged the attentions of the poor men and she has not even been interested in the overtures of some of the rich young men. Boaz has been very impressed. There had apparently been opportunity to encourage towards marriage any number of poor men. And if financial security was really what she was after, then the attentions of the rich young men would have been encouraged. Ruth has not *followedst* the poor or the rich.

She has continued her gleaning to support Naomi and herself and trusts the Lord for her future. Although Boaz has made it clear that he prays for God's blessing in her life and has great admiration for her, he still has not given her an answer. She waits saying nothing.

> *Ruth 3:11 "And now, my daughter, fear not; I will do to thee all that thou requirest: for all the city of my people*

> *doth know that thou art a virtuous woman."*

And Now,

Boaz again speaks. By saying *and now* he introduces a change in what he is going to say. He has been talking about Ruth's character. Character was of first importance to him. He was not concerned with her beauty although she obviously was beautiful. Everyone acknowledges that and especially the young men who were attracted to her.

Neither is he concerned with her lack of financial resources. And he admires the fact that she did not chase after rich men or any men at all for that matter. His admiration of her character is genuine.

My Daughter, Fear Not:

Boaz again addresses Ruth as daughter. He feels protective towards this person he admires so much. He tells her *fear not.* He is telling her not to worry or be concerned about anything. He is telling her to be at peace. She knows only one way that peace, or "rest" as Naomi had phrased it, can be found. In the darkness Ruth begins to feel hope, more hope than she has felt for a very long time. Can it be? Will he? It is amazing how many fragments of thought can run through the mind in a fraction of a second.

I Will Do To Thee All That Thou Requirest.

Yes, Boaz is going to marry Ruth! He does not take long to make up his mind. This may be the result of both his military and civilian careers. He is used to being in charge and making quick judicious decisions. He is a military man when the need arises in Israel and there probably have been many times and many situations in which his life and the lives of the men under him depended upon strategic decisions made quickly. As a wealthy and respected man, in civilian life, he was also a man in authority and used to making decisions on the spot.

Boaz may realize, at this moment, that to marry Ruth, is an attractive idea based on what he already knows about her. He certainly took this attitude in reviewing why he admired her before he told her that he was willing to redeem and marry her. He tells her that he will redeem her as a near kinsman, which is what she has asked of him.

He has said that he *will do* this for her. The Hebrew word for do is asah and again, we have seen this word before. Naomi wanted the Lord to deal (asah) kindly with her daughters-in-law. Ruth wanted the Lord to do (asah) so to her, that is more than kill her if she did not keep her vow to Naomi. And Boaz says he knows what Ruth has done (asah) for her mother-in-law since the death of the husbands. Now Boaz says he will do, or work out, (asah) for her all that she required.

For All The City Of My People

Boaz is stating that what he has said about Ruth is not just his own opinion. All the city of his people (the people of Israel) has come to the same conclusion and they hold the same opinion about her.

He does not hesitate to point out that the people of Bethlehem are his people as opposed to her people. He does not hesitate to indicate that she is a foreigner but it is in the context of his extremely positive opinion of her.

He is saying that while people of other countries may have other standards of conduct, she who has come to trust in the God of Israel, lives by God's standards and the people of the city of Bethlehem recognize that. It is obvious that the inhabitants had discussed thoroughly the topic of Ruth, and Boaz has heard plenty of this discussion. He knows, and this is remarkable since she is still viewed as a foreigner, that she is held in highest regard by *all the city of my people.*

Know That Thou Art A Virtuous Woman.

Again we have the Hebrew word yada, which means to know, to understand, and to perceive. The whole city of Bethlehem is not only of the opinion but actually realizes the fact, knows, that Ruth is *a virtuous woman.* This is an important point that Boaz is making. The vision of a person who is infatuated or who considers himself "in love" can be clouded or distorted. In backing up his opinion with the knowledge of an entire city, Boaz validates his own personal opinion of Ruth.

The Hebrew word used here for virtuous is chayil. It is the same word that was used to describe Boaz in the first mention of him in the beginning of chapter two. There it was translated wealth. The actual meaning for chayil can be translated as both of these words in that the root meaning includes strength, might, valor, wealth, substance, virtue, and honesty. How can this one word represent so many concepts? It all comes together in the Lord. Those who trust in the Lord know that their strength is in the Lord, that all blessings come from the hand of God, that to follow Him requires honest living and a virtuous life. Boaz had already stated that he knew that Ruth trusted in God. It made her the wonderful virtuous woman she was and she radiated this virtue and strength for everyone to see.

Ruth 3:12 "And now it is true that I am thy near kinsman: howbeit there is a kinsman nearer than I."

And Now It Is True That I Am Thy Near Kinsman:

Boaz has already said that he will marry her. He tells Ruth that it is true that he is her kinsman a near kinsman. He agrees that she has a right to call upon him to marry her and redeem their property; the property of Naomi and Ruth.

Howbeit There Is A Kinsman Nearer Than I.

Just when Ruth believes that her future is secure and she will marry this wonderful man, there is a problem that can change everything. Boaz is telling her that although he wants to marry her and thinks very highly of her, this may not be possible. There is another kinsman who has first rights. There is a relative that is a closer relative and therefore he has first claim to her hand.

One wonders why Boaz did not say so in the first place. Why did he let her think, even for a moment, that everything was as good as settled? There may be a couple of possible reasons. He is a gentleman and does not want to make her feel completely disappointed after all her efforts. If it truly was the deepest desire of his heart to marry Ruth then it would be most important to him to reassure her of this fact before he broke the news to her of the problem they would have to face.

Ruth 3:13 "Tarry this night, and it shall be in the morning, that if he will perform unto thee the part of a kinsman, well; let him do the kinsman's part: but if he will not do the part of a kinsman to thee, then will I do the part of a kinsman to thee, as the LORD liveth: lie down until the morning."

Tarry This Night,

Boaz tells Ruth to stay for the rest of the night. It is now dark and it would be difficult for her to find her way home. If Bethlehem was a walled city at this time in history, the city gates would have been closed for the night and it may have been difficult to get into the city.

And It Shall Be In The Morning,

Boaz shows his anxiousness to settle the situation and marry Ruth. He is definitely a man of action. He knows his mind, he has made up his mind, and he will waste no time about it. How romantic, but will love conquer all? Boaz, no doubt, spent a good deal of time (perhaps the rest of the night) thinking about his plan of action and of the lovely Ruth at his feet.

That If He Will Perform Unto Thee The Part Of A Kinsman,

Here is the difficult part. What if the nearer kinsman decides to redeem the land and marry Ruth? Neither of them wanted to think about the possibility and yet it had to be thought of. Would this other person want to marry Ruth? Boaz saw it as a possibility or he would not have given it any thought at all.

Well;

In saying *well,* Boaz means that if the kinsman is willing to redeem the land and marry Ruth then that would be well and good. Ruth and Naomi would have their land redeemed and they would also have a husband to take care of Ruth. It is certainly noble of him to be thinking of Ruth and her need to the abrogation of all his own desires but is this the time for nobility? Apparently it is.

The reason Ruth has given Boaz for her wanting to marry him is that she wants him to perform the part of a kinsman. Even startled out of sleep, he has readily agreed to her desires. He must also admit that there is another who also would no doubt admire what he admires in Ruth and would want to marry her as much as he does (which may or may not be the case but is another sign that Boaz is in love.) If indeed this is the case, that this other person would want to marry Ruth, then Boaz must gracefully bow out and wish her the best.

Let Him Do The Kinsman's Part:

Boaz really has no choice but to allow this other man to claim the hand of Ruth if the other man so desires. It is made all the harder because he sees so much in Ruth that he feels surely everyone and especially this other man will see it too. He has already said that the whole city knows only good of her. It is inconceivable that anyone might not want to marry Ruth as much as he does.

In regards to the nearer kinsman, Boaz does not mention marriage, even though that is what Ruth has asked for. Can it be that he does not want to think of "the other man" marrying Ruth and thus only discusses the part of a kinsman?

Boaz has always shown himself to be brave and never more so than now. And yet, he cannot help but let his heart hope a little as expressed in his next words.

But If He Will Not Do The Part Of A Kinsman To Thee,

Boaz sees that there is, as it were, a small window of opportunity. It is possible, just possible, that the other man may not want to redeem the land and marry Ruth. Boaz will then have his chance. He will be able to redeem the land and marry Ruth.

Then Will I Do The Part Of A Kinsman To Thee,

Boaz again makes his promise to Ruth. If it is not the desire of the other man to redeem the land and marry Ruth and he gives up his rights to do so, then the way will be clear for Boaz and he *will do the part of the kinsman to* Ruth. In saying this, Boaz gives a hint of what will be his strategy.

As The Lord Liveth:

Boaz seals his promise to Ruth with a declaration that as surely as the LORD lives, so too, will he keep his word to her. This is a very strong promise and binds him to Ruth with a solemn vow. The Hebrew word for lives is chay and means life or lives and can also mean live forever.

Just as surely as Ruth could depend upon the fact that the

Lord lives so too could she depend on Boaz to do the part of a kinsman. He has given her an avowal of the strongest possible commitment. It is reminiscent of Ruth's vow of commitment to Naomi. Ruth and Boaz are alike in that both have great strength of character and depth in their love.

Lie Down Until The Morning.

Naomi was right when she said that Boaz would tell her what to do. The plan of action has been settled between them and there is no more need for discussion. Boaz has already begun to take charge of this situation and tells Ruth to *lie down until morning* probably since it is still too dark to see where she is going.

> *Ruth 3:14 "And she lay at his feet until the morning: and she rose up before one could know another. And he said, Let it not be known that a woman came into the floor."*

And She Lay At His Feet Until The Morning:

Ruth went back to the place where she was before at the feet of Boaz. She had placed her future in his hands and had done all that Naomi had told her to do. At any point during the evening and through the night, did she have any misgivings about this plan of Naomi's? There is no indication of it. She trusted the Lord to know what was best for her life. God had brought Naomi into her life in a position of authority and she accepted that. Now Boaz was to have responsibility for her. She trusted in him. There is peace and freedom in trust. Was she able therefore to sleep for the rest of the night? Probably not, she was human after all and there were big changes coming into her life.

And She Rose Up Before One Could Know Another.

Ruth arises before the sun is up, before the earliest birds begin to sing their morning songs. She gets up while it is still so dark that one person could not be clearly distinguished from another. There is only a brief time between total darkness and the breaking of the dawn. If Ruth is going to leave the threshing floor and return to Bethlehem unrecognized she would have to hurry. There was no time to waste. How did she just happen to wake up at precisely the right time? This is another indication that perhaps she just could not sleep with all that has been exchanged between Boaz and herself. Their entire future would soon be decided.

And He Said, Let It Not Be Known That A Woman Came Into The Floor.

Boaz was also awake. Perhaps he could not sleep either. He is aware that Ruth is stirring and is going to leave to go back to Bethlehem. He speaks softly to Ruth. He tells her not to let it be known that a woman had come to the floor. Not only would Boaz prefer that she not be recognized, he also does not want it known that an unknown woman was there during the night.

Having it known that a woman had been with him during the night would only lead to speculation that would put Boaz in a really compromising situation. That kind of news about one of the city's most prominent citizens would be fuel for many a fire and probably not only Boaz would be burnt but Ruth too as soon as everyone learned of their intentions to marry. It was best to avoid even the appearance of evil.

> *Ruth 3:15 "Also he said, Bring the veil that thou hast upon thee, and hold it. And when she held it, he measured six measures of barley, and laid it on her: and she went into the city."*

Also He Said, Bring The Veil That Thou Hast Upon Thee,

Boaz, still speaking very softly, gives Ruth further instructions. He tells her to bring with her the piece of cloth that she has used as a head and face covering. There is no need to hide her face and head as it is dark and no one will recognize her. He quietly tells her to follow him.

And Hold It.

Boaz tells Ruth not to put on her head covering but to hold it in her hand. If she wondered what he meant by this strange request she did not question him.

And When She Held It, He Measured Six Measures Of Barley,

Boaz had Ruth hold out her piece of cloth and he placed barley in the center of it; six measures of barley. A measure, or in Hebrew seah, is equivalent to one-third of an ephah.

Thus, he gave her two ephahs of barley. As seen before, an ephah equals about 6 gallons and three quarts. An ephah was what she had been able to glean on her first day in the field. Now she is given almost 13 gallons of barley. This was an incredible amount and would have been enough to feed Naomi and Ruth for about 100 days if they ate nothing else. It would have been likely that they would have taken some of it to market to sell so they could purchase other necessities.

And Laid It On Her:

Boaz lifted the tied up barley to place it on Ruth. Such a large amount was incredibly heavy and would have been difficult to heft. She is burdened down with so much blessing that it is difficult to carry it all. The first response of Boaz towards Ruth always was and is, generosity. We know that if somehow they are able to marry, this will always be his attitude towards her; to bless her as much as he can. It is a beautiful characteristic to have a generous spirit and Boaz has shown this side of himself once again.

And She Went Into The City.

Ruth returns to Bethlehem with her heavy burden and a happy heart. The most wonderful man in the world who understands her, who has comforted her, who has been generous to her, and cares for her, wants to marry her. There is of course that other man but surely God will work it out for her. She trusts Him. She has seen His loving kindness to her and now in the depths of her heart she has peace even if she may be wondering about how and when it could all work out.

Ruth must have also wondered if Naomi had gotten any sleep. Is she waiting to hear all the details of the fateful evening? Did Naomi know about the other man? There was so much to share and yet it could be summed up in five perfect words. HE WANTS TO MARRY ME!

Part Nine - Ruth Goes Home to Naomi to Await Developments Ruth 3:16 to Ruth 3:18

Ruth 3:16 "And when she came to her mother-in-law, she said, Who art thou, my daughter? And she told her all that the man had done to her."

And When She Came To Her Mother-In-Law,

Ruth made it all the way home with her heavy load. Naomi was waiting for her. The first person she saw was her beloved mother-in-law. Naomi was the one that had planned this all and had instructed her and sent her on her way. After coming away from the man who wanted to marry her, it is Naomi that she wants to talk to.

Her face was not just flushed from toting the heavy load (about eighty pounds) of barley all the way home. A glow of happiness and excitement radiated from her face and it could be clearly seen.

She Said, Who Art Thou, My Daughter?

Naomi saw in an instant that something had happened. Ruth was different. She was more beautiful than ever. She radiated. Naomi asks, *who art thou*? Is this the young woman who left our home a few hours ago? Naomi shows her love for Ruth in persisting in calling her *my daughter.* Ruth's happiness is so evident that Naomi tells her that she looks transformed by her happiness. Ruth does not think of sleep. Maybe she will never want to sleep again. It is so wonderful that she is just bursting to tell Naomi everything.

And She Told Her All That The Man Had Done

The sun would be brightly shining before Ruth came to the end of her tale. Naomi did not miss one detail. She did not miss one little word. It was all too wonderful. Could anyone in the whole world have ever been as happy as Ruth was at this very moment? Naomi asked so many questions and Ruth's excitement was infectious. Both of them exclaimed about the wonders of the man called Boaz. Perhaps Naomi told Ruth all that she remembered about Boaz when he was younger, before she went to Moab.

Ruth *told her all that the man had done.* The Hebrew word for done is asah. We have seen this word several times before including in chapter one verse eight in Naomi's blessing for her two daughters-in-law. Asah was used again in chapter two verse eleven in the blessing of Boaz for Ruth. Its meanings include to do, to work, and to accomplish, as well as to prepare and to handle. The ethical aspect of asah is one of obedience as seen in:

> "Therefore shall ye observe all my statutes, and all my judgments, and do (asah) them: I am the LORD." Leviticus 19:37

Boaz accepted the obligation and responsibility of kinsman-redeemer and had told Ruth he would make the arrangements. Naomi and Ruth went over the details of the incredible night. They went over every detail until all that could be told was told.

To Her.

It was so natural for Ruth to share all her joy and relate all the details *to her,* to Naomi. Naomi could not be happier for Ruth if she had been her own natural daughter. She loved Ruth so much and fully shared in her happiness. And Ruth loved Naomi so much that it was a joy to share everything with her.

> *Ruth 3:17 "And she said, these six measures of barley gave he me; for he said to me, Go not empty unto thy mother-in-law."*

And She Said

Almost as an after thought, Ruth remembers one last thing. It seems incredible that after toting home such a heavy load, that for a while she had forgotten all about it. It shows how excited she was that this heavy, heavy load was forgotten in the telling of the tale.

These Six Measures Of Barley Gave He Me;

Ruth finally remembers all that barley; six whole measures. Ruth now points out to Naomi what she has brought home from the threshing floor and tells Naomi that Boaz has sent her home with it.

For He Said To Me,

Ruth is going to explain why she has come home with all this barley from Boaz. It is a huge gift and Ruth knows that Naomi must wonder about it.

Although Ruth may not be aware of it, this is a very tangible expression of how well Boaz knows Ruth. Ruth may or may not have accepted such a large gift but Boaz knows her heart.

Because of her love for Naomi, Naomi is first and foremost in Ruth's heart. She would be glad to accept a gift for Naomi and Boaz would win her sincere gratitude.

Boaz also knows that this large gift will be a signal to Naomi as to his intentions concerning Ruth. Beyond all this, Boaz wishes to bless this woman he has decided to marry and this is the only suitable gift he has at hand and so he loads Ruth down with almost more than she can carry. Older and wiser heads can see that young lovers can act delightfully foolish.

Go Not Empty Unto Thy Mother-In-Law.

These words had to give Naomi pause for thought. What

did Boaz mean by these words? What did Boaz mean by sending Ruth home with almost more than she could carry? It was incredibly generous but what was the message he was sending with the barley?

Naomi shows by her next words that she perfectly understands the message that Boaz has sent. Boaz knows, as does "all the city," that Ruth is devoted to Naomi and will share with Naomi all that Boaz has said. He also knows that Naomi will know what Boaz is saying with his enormous gift. It is the earnest, the down payment of what is to come.

> *"Ruth 3:18 Then said she, Sit still, my daughter, until thou know how the matter will fall: for the man will not be in rest, until he have finished the thing this day."*

Then Said She,

Naomi realizes what is going to happen, at least to a certain extent. She speaks to Ruth and again tells her what she must do next.

Sit Still My Daughter,

As a mother speaks to her daughter, Naomi knows what is for the best and tells Ruth. This plan of hers seems to be working out and Naomi is still in charge. She tells Ruth to *sit still.* She is telling Ruth that Ruth has done all that there is to be done and now she must just wait and see.

Until Thou Know How The Matter Will Fall:

They must both wait until they know which way the matter will go. The Hebrew word for "know" is yada. Yada is the word used by Boaz when he said that Ruth had come to a people that she did not know (chapter two, verse eleven.)

There has been quite a bit of not knowing in Ruth's life but as Boaz pointed out in the previous use of this word, Ruth may not know what the future holds but she knows, like Job, who holds the future (Job 19:25). Yada is a very important Hebrew root and is used over nine hundred times in the Old Testament. It goes beyond a simple knowing to include understanding, to acquire knowledge, to be familiar with, to inform, to announce, and to reveal oneself. It includes knowing God on a personal basis such as God and Moses knowing each other.

> "And there arose not a prophet since in Israel like unto Moses, whom the LORD knew (yada) face to face," Deuteronomy 34:10

Since Ruth, and of course Naomi, have desired Boaz to marry Ruth on the basis of being a near kinsman and there is a nearer kinsman, the nearer kinsman must be given his chance. The suspense must have been so great and no doubt their minds would never be, very far from wondering how the matter would turn out. If there was ever a time for prayer, this morning was that time.

For The Man Will Not Be In Rest,

Naomi seeks to reassure Ruth and tells her that Boaz will not waste any time. She knows that he will be as anxious as they are to see the outcome and have it settled.

She says *the man will not be in rest.* The Hebrew word used here for rest is shoqat. It has several similar meanings including to be undisturbed, to be inactive, to be calm and to be still. The overall meaning is to be tranquil. Naomi knew that Boaz would have no peace until the whole question of his marrying Ruth was settled.

Until He Have Finished The Thing This Day.

Naomi is fully aware that it is characteristic of Boaz to take his commitment to Ruth very seriously and that he will be anxious to settle the matter as soon as possible. From all that Ruth has reported, since the time of their first meeting in the field until now, Naomi also knows that once Boaz awakened to the realization that Ruth is precisely the right wife for him and that, in fact, he had found her attractive from the very beginning, it was really only an extremely short distance to being deeply in love with this "virtuous" woman.

Naomi also knew that men in love waste no time in planning to make the woman of their desire their own. Thus, it is with the wisdom of an older woman and one who has seen this before, Naomi can confidently state that this very day it will all be settled; one way or the other, it will be settled.

Chapter Four

Part Ten –
Boaz Becomes
Kinsman-redeemer
Ruth 4:1 to Ruth 4:10

Ruth 4:1 "Then went Boaz up to the gate, and sat him down there: and, behold, the kinsman of whom Boaz spake came by; unto whom he said, Ho, such a one! Turn aside, sit down here. And he turned aside, and sat down."

Then Went Boaz Up To The Gate,

Naomi was right. Boaz wasted no time in setting forth to get the matter settled. His adrenalin must have been elevated this morning. Another man had the right to the hand of the woman he wanted to marry. He must be careful.

He had to say the right thing. How best to approach this man without appearing so anxious as to cause the man to want Ruth for himself? If ever he needed to pray and seek the help of the LORD it was now. He decides to go to the gate.

In those days, the city gate was more than a place for people to move in and out of the city. Just inside the gate were judicial buildings that housed the city government. All legal matters were decided here. Business and social contracts were ratified here. These chambers were all referred to as the gate. (No doubt because of the close proximity to the city gate.) It was also a meeting place where one could often find the elders of the city. Sooner or later one was bound to meet everyone at this gathering place so Boaz goes to the gate.

And Sat Him Down There:

Boaz appears cool and collected. He casually sits down. He may have felt like pacing up and down and asking everyone he encounters if they have seen the other kinsman this morning but he does not. He waits. He is a man who trusts the LORD and so he sits down and he waits.

And, Behold,

These same words were used in chapter two and verse four. It was on the occasion of the first appearance of Boaz in the book of Ruth. It was a stop and take note moment. *BEHOLD!* From that very moment, lives would change. Back then, on that day in the field, there was an awareness of the importance of Boaz coming from Bethlehem to the field but only looking back over the years could one see somewhat more clearly how momentous this event really was. And now, we have another *behold.* Make note of this moment. There will be another momentous turn of events.

The Kinsman Of Whom Boaz Spake Came By;

Just as Boaz expected, the nearer kinsman walks by. This is the very man that Boaz had told Ruth about. This is the man who has the right to redeem the property and take Ruth for his bride. When this man walked out of his door this morning he had no idea that he would soon be confronted with having to make a life-changing decision. One way or the other, his decision would change his life forever and it would change the lives of Boaz and Ruth forever too. The man had come by and with him came the direction of the future for all three and Naomi also. His decision will affect the course of all history. He could have no idea of all of this when he came to the gate this fateful morning.

Unto Whom He Said, Ho, Such A One!

Boaz remains at least outwardly calm. He hails the man. In modern vernacular he might have said, "Hey there, you!" It is a friendly, and casual greeting; so casual that he does not even use the man's name. We can see his smile and his motioning for the man to come to where Boaz is sitting and looking for all the world as if he were someone relaxing and watching the world go by without a care or concern on his mind.

Turn Aside, Sit Down Here.

Boaz invites the man to come over and sit down with him.

Sitting down together is much more of a relaxed position than confronting someone standing in the street. Boaz has set the scene for a friendly exchange. He has said in effect, leave what you were about to do and sit with me for a while.

And He Turned Aside, And Sat Down.

We do not know how accustomed the man was to spending time with Boaz. Perhaps they often spent time together since they were relatives. On the other hand, perhaps they were not particularly close and if this was the case, he probably came to sit down out of curiosity. Either way, he did come to sit with Boaz.

> *Ruth 4:2 "And he took ten men of the elders of the city, and said, Sit ye down here. And they sat down."*

And He Took Ten Men Of The Elders Of The City,

Boaz assembles ten of the elders of the city. The elders were the governing body of the city and could often be found sitting in the gate. A quorum of ten of these men was needed to make legal decisions. The Hebrew word here for elder is zaqen and literally means an old man. The practice of having a quorum of ten elders goes clear back to the time of Moses and continued through the monarchy and beyond the time of the exile. Boaz calls ten of these men together who were no doubt nearby.

And Said, Sit Ye Down Here,

Boaz not only called them, he asked them to sit down. Boaz means business; but what business? His relative must have begun to wonder what this was all about. His mind must have raced furiously but he could come to no conclusions.

And They Sat Down.

They were now ready to convene and listen to what Boaz was going to present that needed a legal hearing. These ten men were used to hearing legal proceedings and were probably not too surprised that Boaz had called upon them. They were probably not overly curious and just waited knowing Boaz would explain it in due time.

No doubt the one person probably extremely curious, who clearly did not know what this was all about, was the relative of Boaz. He was perhaps a bit apprehensive as well as astonished that he should be the other party to the question to be decided. What in the world was this all about? The elders sat down and Boaz was ready to begin.

> *Ruth 4:3 "And he said unto the kinsman, Naomi, that is come again out of the country of Moab, selleth a parcel of land, which was our brother Elimelech's:"*

And He Said Unto The Kinsman,

Boaz turns to the nearer kinsman and speaks directly to his relative, this nearer kinsman of Naomi. Now the nearer kinsman knows for sure that there is something that Boaz wants to settle between them. Boaz is speaking to the nearer kinsman but also in the presence of the elders, so that, what he says will be heard by them.

Naomi That Is Come Again Out Of The Country Of Moab,

Boaz begins by mentioning Naomi. He does not open his presentation with the fact that he wishes to marry Ruth, which is what is behind all of this. He starts out by talking about Naomi. He mentions that she is the Naomi that has come back from Moab, ostensibly, in case she should be confused with any other Naomi. It is also a reminder that she left Bethlehem and thus Boaz is bringing out an incident in their family that does not enhance the family image. An ever so slightly negative tone has been introduced.

We can see everyone nodding his head. Everyone knows about Naomi and her return from Moab. Going to Moab had been a disaster for her. She was now destitute and with a dependent. The whole city has been engrossed with all the details of her story. The ten elders and the relative all know about Naomi. They wait for more.

Selleth A Parcel Of Land,

Boaz informs them all that Naomi wishes to sell a parcel of land (fifteenth use of the word sadeh.) Her husband's land is now hers to dispose of if she wishes. Everyone knows that Naomi has fallen on hard times and in order to have some money to live on it makes perfect sense to everyone that she would wish to sell some of her land.

Which Was Our Brother Elimelech's:

Things begin to become a little clearer and perhaps the nearer kinsman begins to think he knows where this is going. By stating that Elimelech is their brother, Boaz is not saying that the three men have the same mother and father. He uses the term brother in the broader sense; they are of the same larger family. More to the point, he is saying that we have a right to redeem the parcel before anyone else can come forward and make an offer on the land.

In fact, Boaz knows that his relative realizes that Boaz is actually second in line and that he is first. Speaking in terms that might be interpreted as a willingness to share family responsibility adds to the feeling of camaraderie and esprit de corps between them. Boaz continues to speak to his relative in front of the elders.

> *Ruth 4:4 "And I thought to advise thee, saying, Buy it before the inhabitants, and before the elders of my people. If thou wilt redeem it, redeem it: but if thou wilt not redeem it, then tell me, that I may know: for there is none to redeem it besides thee; and I am after thee. And he said, I will redeem it."*

And I Thought To Advise Thee,

Boaz is telling his relative that the reason he has asked him to come and sit with him is that he wishes to inform him of the intentions of Naomi. It was a really decent thing to do and this must make the relative feel some gratitude and good will towards Boaz. No doubt the elders also feel that Boaz has acted the part of a gentleman and has done the right thing.

Saying, Buy It Before The Inhabitants,

Boaz is not only advising the man about the fact that Naomi wishes to sell her property, but, he goes further and tells him to buy it. This may seem like a generous offer of information with the advice to buy the property and thereby doing the right thing by the destitute Naomi. But it also takes the decision away from the kinsman in that he is now placed in the position of only following the directive of Boaz and not making an independently generous decision on his own. If he does decide to buy the property, it is Boaz who will also get the accolades and not just him because it was Boaz's idea and directive for him to buy the property in the first place.

Boaz now subtly applies a little pressure. Apparently not only are the elders of the city listening to all that Boaz is relating, but also many others of the inhabitants of Bethlehem. The gate after all is the local gathering place. Boaz is taking advantage of the spectators crowded around to listen to the proceedings. As well as being witnesses to what the nearer kinsman will decide, these inhabitants become a visual image of the inhabitants of the city crowded around and ready to pounce on the opportunity to buy Naomi's property if the nearer kinsman declines. This kinsman had better buy the property *before the inhabitants* have their chance to do so and in plain view of them before the opportunity is lost forever.

And Before The Elders Of My People.

Boaz applies a little more pressure. He is saying, let us settle the matter right now since we have here the elders that will allow us to make the whole thing legally settled. Adding the phrase *my people,* almost imperceptibly, shifts the weight of legality to the side of Boaz before the nearer relative even has the chance to perceive that he and Boaz are not two comrades in league as "brothers" in the same family but actually contenders. As Boaz's people they would naturally be on his side but who is asking for sides to be taken? It is strictly below the surface but on reflection the nearer relative would realize that these elders are of his people too. The nearer relative does not have time for reflection. Something else is on the table for consideration and that is the question of whether he wishes to purchase the plot of land from Naomi or not.

If Thou Wilt Redeem It, Redeem It:

For a third time, the pressure builds a little more. Boaz tells the nearer relative, if you are going to do it, do it. Having had little time to consider, the nearer relative is almost forced to make an immediate decision. To waffle at this point would be embarrassing in front of the ten pairs of eyes fastened on his face and waiting for his answer.

Then Tell Me

It seems that Boaz is only making a reasonable request. He will even give a perfectly understandable reason for his request but nevertheless it once again adds just a little more pressure.

That I May Know:

Boaz is saying that the reason for asking his relative to come aside and sit down and the reason he has asked the elders to also come is that he has a need to know what the near relative wishes to do concerning the parcel of land that Naomi wants to sell. By implication, Boaz is saying that the near relative needs to make a decision because it otherwise will cause a problem for Boaz. He needs to know. Boaz will make it clear why he needs to know but meanwhile once again this need to know adds even more pressure for the nearer relative to make a decision.

For There Is None To Redeem It Besides Thee;

This very last reason for once more applying yet more pressure is justified by the heartbreaking thought that Naomi is alone in the world, adrift on a sea of grief and poverty, with not an anchor to hold her or anyone besides this near kinsman to bring her safely to shore.

The fact that Naomi has land to sell to sustain her does not enter this poignant picture. Boaz goes on to say that this is not only about Naomi, but, really, it is about keeping the land in the family. This was not only a question of ethic but also of edict.

When the children of Israel entered the land of promise, God gave each family specific areas of land. It was not to be sold outside of the family. Thus, Naomi needs a relative to buy the land so it can stay in the family and Boaz is pointing out that this relative is Naomi's nearest and only hope; there is no one else.

And I Am After Thee.

Boaz qualifies his last statement by adding the fact that, of course, he himself comes after his relative in the very short list of those who have the right of redemption. Dare we say that this little rider also adds pressure? Without dwelling on the obvious pressure, it is apparent that if the relative refuses to purchase the property then in order to follow the commandment of the Lord, he will in effect be forcing Boaz to purchase the property. We can see the elders, if not physically, at least mentally shaking their heads. Poor kindly Boaz will be put upon because this nearer kinsman will not fulfill his duty.

And He Said,

The nearer relative has listened to all that Boaz has said in front of these ten men. Boaz has shared with him the situation and the need for a decision. It would be a wonder if he did not feel somewhat like he had been boxed into a corner; not of course by this friendly relative. Boaz had only asked him to sit down so they could solve this unexpected family question of redemption. It was caused by the urgency of the situation.

He has to decide if he wants to buy the land and if he can afford it. If he decides against purchasing it, he realizes that he has placed the same decision on Boaz. That would be a little awkward since it was first and foremost his responsibility and would only fall to Boaz if he refused to meet his responsibility in this situation. It was not the fault of Boaz that Naomi needed to sell a parcel of land and that he just happened to be the nearer kinsman. There was probably not a man among the ten who did not expect him to step forward and buy the land. The nearer relative realizes that yes, it is necessary to make a decision and so he does.

I Will Redeem It.

How could Boaz let this happen? The "other man" has been almost forced by Boaz to buy the land. What can he have been thinking? This does not make any sense at all. He wants to marry Ruth, he really does. What has he done? What has all this to do with settling Ruth's future anyway?

> *Ruth 4:5 "Then said Boaz, What day thou buyest the field of the hand of Naomi, thou must also buy it of Ruth the Moabitess, the wife of the dead, to raise up the name of the dead upon his inheritance."*

Then Said Boaz,

Boaz has one more thing to say. Just when it seemed that everything had gone a long way to being settled, Boaz has one more thing to say.

What Day Thou Buyest The Field Of The Hand Of Naomi,

We have in this verse the sixteenth and final use of the word sadeh or field. These last two uses refer not only to a place in Bethlehem but cause the balance of reference to living in Moab and living in Israel to be weighted in favor of Israel. (There were seven references to the fields of Moab and now nine to the fields of Israel.) It is interesting that it is Naomi's land that settles the difference once and for all. We see a foreshadowing of the fact that coming back home to her own field will bring her to a place of blessing from the Lord.

At the gate, there is something important that will occur on the very day that the purchase of Naomi's land (sadeh) is made. Boaz is about to point out the facts of the matter since the nearer kinsman may have overlooked them.

Thou Must Also Buy It Of Ruth

Boaz is pointing out that Ruth is also connected to the land. As the wife of the son of Elimelech who would have inherited the land from his father, she also has rights to it.

The Moabitess,

In using the words *the Moabitess* as if it were part of her given name, Boaz may just be using the appellation given to Ruth by the citizens of Bethlehem. He may also be taking this opportunity to remind the nearer kinsman that Ruth is a Moabitess. Since the Moabites, in general, are given bad press, this is not in Ruth's favor and Boaz's bending to popular parlance does not help to paint Ruth in a favorable light in the mind of the nearer kinsman.

The Wife Of The Dead,

Boaz again may be simply pointing out that the husband of Ruth who would have inherited the property, should he have lived and come back, now gives, in death, the rights to what he would have inherited to Ruth. On the other hand, intentionally or unintentionally, Boaz conjures up a morbid picture. There is a natural repugnance to death and to bring up the image of a beautiful woman married to a corpse is not pleasant even if the image is only a briefly subconscious one.

To Raise Up The Name Of The Dead Upon His Inheritance.

Boaz is telling the nearer kinsman that, if he wants to purchase the property, the price tag includes marriage to Ruth. He will have to marry Ruth with the view of having a son who would one day inherit the property in the name of Ruth's dead husband. Whether consciously or unconsciously, Boaz has done his best.

The nearer kinsman has already been almost forced to make an uncomfortably hasty decision concerning a large investment. He has also been almost forced to accept unlooked for responsibility, concerning keeping the property in the family. He has been intimidated by having to make this precipitant decision and almost forced acceptance of responsibility by the staring presence of ten highly respected elders of the community, not to mention all these other obviously interested bystanders.

For a moment only, he is allowed to feel that he has acted honorably and perhaps even nobly, in agreeing to redeem the property. Now he is told that he will have to marry the foreign wife of a dead man so that their hoped for first-born son could inherit from this dead man what he, the nearer kinsman, is about to pay for.

Was there incredulity written in his face with the dawning understanding of what was being asked of him? What will he now decide to do? Boaz, at this point, must have joined the others in staring into his face trying to read his decision there. The happiness of not only Boaz, but also of Ruth hung in the balance. Was it an eternity before the nearer kinsman made up his mind? Boaz no doubt thought so.

Ruth 4:6 "And the kinsman said, I cannot redeem it for myself, lest I mar mine own inheritance: redeem thou my right to thyself; for I cannot redeem it."

And The Kinsman Said,

Before all the ten elders, the kinsman gives his answer, making it binding and legal. He has not had a great deal of time to consider so he must follow his instincts and immediate judgment on this spur of the moment decision.

I Cannot Redeem It For Myself,

The kinsman has made his decision. He has changed his mind about the property. Apparently, the idea of marrying Ruth was what tilted the balance. Perhaps Boaz let out the breath he did not even know he was holding, but he did it quietly. He had been gracious and friendly with his kinsman in letting him know that Naomi wanted to sell a parcel of land. He no doubt continued in the same vein. There was no need to let the kinsman know that he was ecstatic beyond words.

No one seems to notice the implications of this kinsman deciding not to make the purchase. Boaz has kept the focus on the land. The whole discussion had revolved around the land. That is what was important. The whole thing about marrying the Moabite widow was a side issue. Granted it was the deciding point but still in the minds of probably everyone, (everyone except Boaz), a side issue.

Boaz had guided the discussion along this line and it never jumped track. He has stated that he would purchase the land if the nearer kinsman declined to do so. Everyone knew that Naomi had come back destitute and it was no wonder that she wanted to sell the land. If anyone thought about the implications of Boaz's willingness to purchase the property, it would be seen as an act of kindness on the part of a wealthy man. It would be seen as just one more act of benevolence on the part of Boaz in their community. Word had no doubt already gotten around about how he had "helped" in Ruth's gleaning. He was a kind man.

With all this talk about the land, it was easy to focus on that, rather than the idea that if the nearer kinsman declines to marry Ruth, then Boaz is going to marry her. With the nearer kinsman declining to marry Ruth, the fact that Boaz was willing to do so made him look virtually heroic.

It was not quite over yet. The nearer kinsman continues to speak.

Lest I Mar My Own Inheritance:

The explanation that the nearer kinsman gives for not redeeming the land as well as not marrying Ruth, is that it will somehow degrade his own inheritance. It is difficult to see just what he is getting at but there are several possibilities.

First, he may not have felt financially comfortable in making a purchase of land at this point but had felt forced into it by the pressure of his sense of moral responsibility. Boaz had stated that he would purchase the land if the kinsman did not. The need to keep the land in the family and thus fulfilling the requirement of God would be met. It would not be to the nearer kinsman's discredit if he simply could not afford to redeem the land.

If the nearer kinsman felt that the purchase of the land would stretch him financially, since it was only the beginning of the new agricultural year's harvest, then taking a wife (let alone her being someone's widow and also a foreigner) could be a financial disaster.

Another possibility for reluctance to redeem the land and marry Ruth may be that he did not actually have the funds. If he had to mortgage his own property in order to purchase the property of Naomi, then it might jeopardize what he had inherited from his father; his inheritance. All it would take is one lean year (along with the added expense of a wife) when he could not pay the mortgage and he could end up losing both properties.

He could have also been thinking farther down the road to his second son. First sons inherited a double portion of the estate. If some of the resources of the nearer kinsman's estate were to go into buying Naomi's property, the first son would still inherit his double portion of what was left as well as the property purchased from Naomi, thus diminishing the second son's inheritance from the nearer kinsman.

There are probably more scenarios to explain the nearer kinsman's explanation of marring his inheritance but whatever he actually was thinking of, the fact remains, he declined to purchase the property and marry Ruth.

Redeem Thou My Right To Thyself;

It almost sounds like the nearer kinsman is issuing a challenge. Whether uttered with a calm friendly smile or an almost angry "anyone can see I am justified" tone of voice, the nearer kinsman not only declines but also challenges Boaz to redeem the property.

If these ten men think it shameful for him not to redeem the property then the shame will have to rest on Boaz too if he does not keep his word. Boaz is right behind him in responsibility to buy the property. And come to think of it, it was Boaz who brought this to the attention of all these elders. Naomi could have sold the property to anyone and there might have been a little talk but he would have had the honest excuse of never even knowing she needed to sell a piece of land.

But now that Boaz has brought all these elders into it, it is bound to create a lot of talk and he, as the nearer kinsman will be thought derelict in his duty. Everyone is going to be looking at him as the one who failed to fulfill his obligations. If Boaz also backs out, Boaz will not be seen as the one who did not fulfill his responsibility so much as the nearer kinsman. He, as nearer kinsman bears first responsibility after all. It did not seem fair. If anyone was going to get blamed for not doing his duty, well it was not going to be just him. Let Boaz sit there looking as if he was full of righteous concern. Was he really so concerned? All right, let him marry the Moabite widow. And if Boaz did not want to marry her either, then that would go a long way to justifying anyone else who had declined. Surely he had made the right decision and was glad of it.

For I Cannot Redeem It.

The nearer kinsman firmly finalizes his decision by again reiterating what he has already said. *I cannot redeem it.* Once and for all, once and forever, it is settled.

> *Ruth 4:7 "Now this was the manner in the former time in Israel concerning redeeming and concerning changing, for to confirm all things; a man plucked off his shoe, and gave it to his neighbor: and this as a testimony in Israel."*

Now This Was The Manner In The Former Time In Israel

We have, here in the text, an explanation of a custom that had passed out of use. By the time the account of the story found in the book of Ruth was written down, customs had changed and therefore this older, *former,* custom had to be explained.

Concerning Redeeming And Concerning Changing, For To Confirm All Things;

This custom, which will be explained, concerned the confirming documentation of redeeming and other legal settlements. It was used to provide validation of the transaction. Today we have notarized documents and raised government seals on such documents as marriage certificates, birth certificates and so forth.

A Man Plucked Off His Shoe And Gave It To His Neighbor:

The custom was to give a shoe as a legal token of the agreement. They gave more than their word; they gave the shoe off their foot. It is not clear how this custom arose. We can see similar affirmation today, in the expression, "you can stand on that." It is an expression that pledges that a person can have complete trust in the word of the speaker. In those days, as a physical sign of certified documentation you actually had not only his word to stand on you also had his shoe.

A neighbor is the person being dealt with or one who is standing closest because he is the one who is partner in the transaction. In other words, the person with whom the agreement is being made.

And This As A Testimony In Israel.

The purpose of this custom was to have a physical testimony or evidence, to the agreement. It also drew out the agreement process in a much more dramatic way. A mere yes-yes, even in front of ten men, would, in time, be much more open to interpretation than the taking off of a shoe and passing it to the other person.

Memory is a very tricky thing. If the party was very reluctant to say yes to begin with, years later the reluctance might be more remembered than the actual yes and there could arise doubt that he ever actually said yes. Having a person sit and unlace a shoe and hand it over would be very memorable, let alone having the physical evidence of the shoe itself. As the custom dictated, they would have *this as a testimony in Israel.*

> *Ruth 4:8 "Therefore the kinsman said unto Boaz, Buy it for thee. So he drew off his shoe."*

Therefore The Kinsman Said Unto Boaz, Buy It For Thee.

The kinsman has already explained that he cannot buy the property because along with marrying Ruth, it would put his inheritance in jeopardy. *Therefore, the kinsman said unto Boaz,* go ahead and buy it yourself.

So He Drew Off His Shoe.

In finality, to finish this whole discussion of whether he will buy the property or not, the nearer kinsman relinquishes his right to do so and forever closes the discussion and abrogates his rights to redeem the property at any time in the future by taking off his shoe.

> *Ruth 4:9 "And Boaz said unto the elders, and unto all the people, Ye are witnesses this day, that I have bought all that was Elimelech's, and all that was Chilion's and Mahlon's, of the hand of Naomi."*

And Boaz Said Unto The Elders,

Boaz concludes the proceedings by addressing the elders. These men are the legal body who will validate the transaction that Boaz wishes to make.

And Unto All The People,

It is apparent that a larger audience had continued to stay and listen throughout the proceedings. We do not know if the "courthouse" was packed, but people had gathered to hear what was going forward. No doubt, by evening the whole city would know what was in the works.

Ye Are Witnesses

Boaz wanted everyone to know that he was going to assume the responsibility of kinsman redeemer. He tells the elders as well as the whole group that has assembled, that they *are witnesses this day.* In so doing he makes them a party to what is going to happen. This is now a community event involving everyone.

This Day,

Boaz seeks to impresses upon the group that they are to know that *this day* they have become party to the fact that indeed he is the kinsman redeemer. This day they have been a party to a change in history. Little did even Boaz know how important this ordinary day was and how a not so extraordinary event would alter all of world history. On *this day* they were witnesses.

That I Have Bought All That Was Elimelech's,

Boaz, as kinsman redeemer, is buying from Naomi not just a parcel of land but all the property that had belonged to Elimelech. All the land that had provided sustenance and income for Elimelech and his family would now belong to Boaz. It was settled this day.

And All That Was Chilion's And Mahlon's,

Boaz makes it clear that he will redeem all the property of Elimelech. Boaz will redeem even the claims that the sons would have had after the death of their father. It is interesting that, Boaz will redeem the title of all the family property. In his promise to redeem *all that was Chilion's and Mahlon's*, Chilion is mentioned first before Mahlon in this redeeming.

In the first mention of the two sons in chapter one and verse two, Mahlon was mentioned first and presumed to be the elder. They are again mentioned in death with Mahlon again first in chapter one verse five. Since Mahlon died first then Chilion was the last holder of the right to the property

Although neither son chose to come back from Moab to claim their inheritance after the death of their father, they would still have been the rightful owners. If Orpah had remarried, as Naomi assumed she would, then she would be out of the picture and actually she is out of the picture already since she did not come back with Naomi. Ruth, of course has some right to the property, but as long as Naomi lives and Ruth is single, she is second to Naomi's right to the property.

Boaz needs to redeem Chilion's right to the property first since Chilion was the last living owner and therefore the last rightful male heir. Naomi has prior rights before Ruth since Naomi was married to the first owner among the three men as the wife of Elimelech.

> *Ruth 4:10 "Moreover Ruth the Moabitess, the wife of Mahlon, have I purchased to be my wife, to raise up the name of the dead upon his inheritance, that the name of the dead be not cut off from among his brethren, and from the gate of his place: ye are witnesses this day."*

Moreover Ruth The Moabitess,

Boaz at last speaks of Ruth who indeed is not only at the center of this whole scene at the gate; she is the reason for the scene. In mentioning her again, with reference to the fact that she is not of Israel and is indeed a foreigner, Boaz not only faces this fact openly, he forces everyone else to face it also. It opens, to public forum, the possibility and opportunity, of objection from the outset. It is reminiscent of the clause in our modern wedding ceremonies that says, if anyone can show just cause as to why this man and this woman should not be married let him now speak or forever hold his peace. No one spoke.

The Wife Of Mahlon,

Boaz is not trying to make clear Ruth's identity by way of explaining that the Ruth he is talking about is the one who was married to Mahlon. What he is pointing out is that she was *the wife of Mahlon* and that is why what he is going to say is important. Identity is not the issue; relationship is the issue.

Have I Purchased To Be My Wife,

Not knowing the customs of the day, it is impossible to say for sure, but it sounds as if there were some sort of bride price to pay and Boaz has done that. What is more important is what he states as his reason for doing so.

To Raise Up The Name Of The Dead Upon His Inheritance,

It was important in Israel to remember the names of the ancestors who had passed away in connection to each piece of land that had been given to them by God. These names represented the lives of people; people who lived lives of righteousness before the LORD and sometimes others who did not. Ancestry gave inheritance for the ownership of the land. Spiritual inheritance gave either blessings or curses on the lives of descendants. With both, physical and spiritual inheritance, it was important that the name of the dead and the memory of his life be continued. It was also necessary that the family line be continued in order to maintain God's gift of family property.

That The Name Of The Dead Be Not Cut Off

Boaz knew that it was important that the family of Elimelech not be wiped out. He is a responsible person and he takes his responsibilities seriously. It has already been established that Boaz is next in line as the person responsible to redeem the property. He also knows that the community will be watching to see what he will do.

All of Israel knows that it is important to keep the land in the family of the original owner. This has a dual action. The redeemer will hopefully have a son so that he can carry on the name on the deed that the redeemer has purchased. In this way the name and lineage of the person connected to this particular piece of property will be preserved in order to validate present ownership. This preserves not only the history of lineage but also the legitimacy of ownership of the property for the son. Meanwhile, the redeemer has the benefit of the property for many years in the income it produces.

Boaz tells the people gathered (and by extension the

whole community) that he will redeem all the land of Elimelech, marry Ruth, and hopefully raise a son to inherit the land. Today this future son might be given a hyphenated surname to represent both families. In those days a person had only his own name but was often further identified as the son of so and so.

From Among His Brethren,

If Elimelech were to be cut off from among his brethren, it would mean that he would no longer have any social recognition or rights in the community. The fact that Elimelech is dead does not enter into consideration because Elimelech is more than an individual. He is a family. A family that still lives represents him. If he were to be cut off it would mean that his family was cut off, that is, there would be no descendants to hold a piece of the covenant promised land.

And From The Gate Of His Place:

His place, that is the place of Elimelech, is Bethlehem. The legacy is tied to Bethlehem; the people (brethren) and the very ground. As we have seen, the gate of a city was where all legal matters were convened. If Elimelech was cut off from the gate, it would mean that having no descendants the family would legally be wiped out. All and any rights to the land would no longer exist. Boaz is saying he does not want any of this to happen and that is the reason for what he has decided to do; that is to say, to redeem the land and marry Ruth and hopefully have a son.

Ye Are Witnesses This Day.

Boaz has declared that all who have gathered to hear what is going forward are now witnesses to the fact that he has decided to redeem the land and marry Ruth and that the nearer kinsman has agreed to this. This is a day he wants them to remember. Although no one yet realizes it, this is the day that changed history for their descendents, for all of Israel and for all of us. *Ye are witnesses this day.*

Part Eleven – The Elders, People, and Women Bless the Marriage Ruth 4:11 to Ruth 4:12

Ruth 4:11 "And all the people that were in the gate, and the elders, said, We are witnesses. The LORD make the woman that is come into thine house like Rachel and like Leah, which two did build the house of Israel: and do thou worthily in Ephratah, and be famous in Bethlehem:"

And All The People That Were In The Gate, And The Elders, Said,

In one accord, the people agreed. They agreed with what Boaz wanted to do. They agreed to his redeeming the land. They agreed to his wanting to marry the widow of

Mahlon. And they agreed to his desire to raise-up the name of Elimelech.

We Are Witnesses.

Everyone present there decided that they individually and collectively would be glad to confirm the justice and rightness of what Boaz freely stated he has done. They agreed and said *we are witnesses.*

The LORD Make The Woman That Is Come Into Thine House Like Rachel And Like Leah,

The elders and people now declare a blessing on the union of Boaz and Ruth. They pray that the LORD will bless Ruth and Boaz with children. They pray that Ruth will be like both Rachel and Leah. These two women were the mothers of the men who were the fathers (progenitors) of the twelve tribes of Israel. These sons of Rachel and Leah were also for whom the tribes of Israel were named.

Ruth is referred to here as the woman rather than by her name. The elders and people were not negating Ruth as a person but rather refer to her function as a wife to Boaz. It is about Boaz and their wishes for him. He is, after all, the person whose intentions they have been called upon to validate. They are not only validating the redeeming of the property and marriage, they are heartily blessing it.

Which Two Did Build The House Of Israel:

Clearly, the credit for the building of the house of Israel goes to the mothers of Israel. Everyone recognizes and is in agreement with this fact. It is a reason to rejoice in motherhood and to expectantly rejoice with Boaz and Ruth. It is given to women to conceive or not to conceive, and bare children. While it is impossible for a woman to conceive without the seed of man, it is nevertheless the woman who does the conceiving and bares a child. The people all pray that Ruth will conceive and bare many children. There was much good will behind this blessing on the part of the community towards Boaz and Ruth.

And Do Thou Worthily In Ephratah,

Once again we have reference to Ephratah, the old name for Bethlehem, and we are reminded that Boaz is of an old established family. He is being encouraged in this new phase of life to do worthily, to be worthy of being a part of this old and respected family. It is similar to advice that may be given to any newlywed as he starts out in his wedded life as a husband.

Boaz is a part of the Bethlehem community and they encourage him to set out on a course that will bring honor to himself, his family, and his community. Boaz is given a command, a charge, and a commission. His command is to *do* and it is personalized with the word thou (or you.) The elders were wise men. For Boaz, fulfillment in his life is fulfilling God's plan for his life. Leading a full life, with the woman God had chosen for him by his side, would not just happen. It would take a listening heart and a conscious effort to do God's will. All that he does will affect more than his own life. He will have a wife and eventually children to consider. What he does will affect them and generations to come. The elders were telling him that marriage is a serious business and not to be entered into lightly.

After the command to do there is a charge. The charge is

to always act in such a way as is worthy; that is, he is to *do thou worthily.* Boaz is told that he should act in such a way as to bring respect and honor in all he does. He is to act in a fitting way that lives up to his position as a husband, father (eventually) and esteemed member of the community. He is to act with integrity; that is *worthily.*

And finally he is given a commission. This respect and honor is not to be brought only or even particularly to himself, but more importantly, to Ephratah, He is to continue the high and worthy position of his antecedents who were Ephrathites. Boaz has been blessed in his heritage and with worthy actions he will be able to pass this blessing on down to his descendants.

This is a challenging command, charge and commission but the community is behind him to support him and is no doubt ready to give their opinions and advice on an ongoing basis. They obviously have faith in him to accomplish all that they have set before him.

And Be Famous In Bethlehem:

It is inspiring to think of goals for the future. The elders knew that one has to have goals in order to reach those goals. Along with considering past heritage and looking into the distant future there is life to be lived in the here and now. The elders encourage Boaz to *be famous in Bethlehem.* Boaz is living in the present, in Bethlehem and he is encouraged to be famous, to be so outstanding in what he does that it will be remarkable and remarked upon. He will be famous.

> *Ruth 4:12 "And let thy house be like the house of Pharez, whom Tamar bare unto Judah, of the seed which the*

LORD shall give thee of this young woman."

And Let Thy House Be Like The House Of Pharez,

The elders pronounce a blessing upon Boaz. They pray that he will have many descendants, as did his ancestor Pharez. The elders are saying that they wish for Boaz a similar multiplication of his family.

Whom Tamar Bare Unto Judah,

The story of the birth of Pharez was well known to Boaz and all of the land of Judah. In fact, Boaz was not only from the tribe of Judah, he was also a descendant of Pharez as were probably a great majority, if not all, of the inhabitants of Bethlehem. Judah was one of the twelve sons of Jacob and thus when the Promised Land was apportioned, part of it was set aside, for the descendants of Judah. One of his sons was named Pharez.

Judah had several sons. After marriage, one of his sons died childless. Judah promised the young widow, Tamar, that as soon as a younger brother was old enough, that she could marry him. This would be another example of the parent arranging the marriage. It would also be an example of a goel marriage. The younger son would be the kinsman redeemer so that Tamar could have a son not only to preserve the name of her dead husband and keep his share of the property in the family, but also so she would have someone to provide and care for her in her old age.

Judah did not make good on his promise, for whatever reason, so Tamar set a trap for him. She heard that he would be out of town on business. His wife had just died so perhaps this was a good reason to get away for a brief time. Tamar covered her face and waited along the road pretending to be a prostitute. Judah saw her and propositioned her, not recognizing her as his daughter-in-law. He promised to send her a kid from his flock. She agreed to the payment but she said she wanted a pledge. He asked her what she wanted as a pledge and she said she wanted his signet, his bracelets, and his staff. Judah agreed.

Afterwards, Tamar went back home (not waiting for the kid.) She soon found out that she had conceived the child she had wanted. When Judah heard that his daughter-in-law was pregnant he was angry and wanted her dead because she had been acting like a prostitute with some unknown man. He felt she deserved death for "playing the harlot." Tamar produced the signet, the bracelets, and the staff and said the father of her baby was the owner of these things. Judah said that he had acted worse than she had and that was the end of his desire to see her dead. Tamar bore not one son but twins and the firstborn was Pharez.

Of The Seed Which The Lord Shall Give Thee

The elders are not just looking at the children that Boaz will have, but also the generations to come. They are praying that his descendants will be many in the years to come, just as Pharez has had many descendants including, of course, Boaz. They are calling on the Lord to do this for Boaz because they acknowledge that it is the LORD alone who will cause this to happen.

Of This Young Woman.

The elders recognize that all the blessings will come

through his marriage to *this young woman,* to Ruth. They approve of his marrying Ruth and give them their blessing.

Part Twelve – The Marriage is Blessed with a Child and the Kingly Line Revealed Ruth 4:13 to Ruth 4:22

Ruth 4:13 "So Boaz took Ruth, and she was his wife: and when he went in unto her, the LORD gave her conception, and she bare a son."

And So Boaz Took Ruth,

The focus of this passage is still on Boaz and what he said, what was said to him, and now what he did. There may have been some questions about why Boaz would marry a woman from Moab. While women from Moab had the reputation of being beautiful, and Ruth was lovely, still there is a tendency to feel negative about all Moabites. Why then, as an outstanding member of the community, fully aware of his position of responsibility, would Boaz show no hesitancy in marrying a Moabitess?

The answer may run deep in the blood of his veins. While the father of Boaz was an Israelite, his mother was none other than the brave and daring Rahab of Jericho. It is true, in fact, that the mother of Boaz was a foreigner. She had come to trust in the Lord and was a convert but a foreigner nevertheless and with a dubious past, to say the least.

There was probably none better in Bethlehem to understand what Ruth's transplant among strangers meant to her. She had already been so grateful for his understanding and acting towards her in a friendly way. It has become clear that this was a marriage made quite literally in heaven. And to make things even better, Boaz has not only the acceptance of his community for this marriage, but also their blessing and good will. He has done an excellent thing (something another was unwilling to do) in wanting to redeem the land and marry Ruth. Boaz has their approval.

So Boaz took Ruth. We still have these words in our wedding ceremonies today; "I... take you...", and they are still words of a promise and a covenant.

And She Was His Wife:

Ruth has also made her promise and commitment to Boaz and has married him. She had to be very happy. Once she faced a future of dwindling into old age in poverty and loneliness. She had vowed to Naomi to stay here for the rest of her life even after the death of Naomi. There was nothing to look forward to except loneliness and misery. Now all that has changed. God really does answer the prayers of even seemingly insignificant people. In fact, Ruth now knows that even the lowliest person is not insignificant to God. And now she was married. She was the wife of the man she loved. It must have been hard to believe that life could be so good. She, imagine that, was married to the most wonderful man in the world. She was married to Boaz.

And When He Went In Unto Her, The LORD Gave Her Conception,

Boaz and Ruth consummate their marriage and God gave her conception. God gave Ruth a miracle. There have been many prayers in this book by a variety of people and we have seen prayers answered and the unfolding of God's plans in the lives of these people. This, however, is now a second time when we are actually told that God acts in a very overt way. The first time was when God intervened on behalf of the whole country to end the famine, which had lasted for many years. Now again we have a direct intervention on the part of God. God gives Ruth conception.

And She Bare A Son.

The greatest blessing God can bestow upon a couple is a child. The marriage of Ruth and Boaz is blessed with a precious baby. As we look into his tiny face with them we wonder what his life will hold; what will this little son be like when he has grown up. As each day passes they learn more things about him and the little person he is at even this early stage. Ruth and Boaz have a son. Now more than ever they can understand the love the Father has for them.

Back when the Israelites were slaves in Egypt, God told Moses what to say when he stood before Pharaoh:

"And thou shalt say unto Pharaoh, Thus saith

> the LORD, Israel is my son, even my first-born:" Exodus 4:22

Yes, with the birth of their son, Ruth and Boaz can see more clearly the love that God has for them. This could happily be the end of a delightful story but it is not because more lives are affected by the birth of this child than just the lives of Ruth and Boaz and Naomi.

> *Ruth 4:14 "And the women said unto Naomi, Blessed be the LORD, which hath not left thee this day without a kinsman, that his name may be famous in Israel."*

And The Women Said Unto Naomi,

The women of Bethlehem see the deeper significance of this birth. The whole of Bethlehem has heard the story of the family of Elimelech and have shown great interest in what has happened to Naomi. They have heard about the redemption of the property and the marriage of Boaz and Ruth. They have seen Naomi go from being full to being empty and now her life has changed once again to being full. Knowing all that has happened they have come to share in her joy.

Blessed Be The LORD,

The first thing they do is to praise the LORD. *Blessed be the LORD.* They know that the hand of God has been on all that has happened in the life of Naomi and Ruth and Boaz.

They are thankful on behalf of each of them that God has done this wonderful thing in giving the family a child. They all recognize this and say, *blessed be the LORD.*

Which Hath Not Left Thee This Day Without A Kinsman,

The women of Bethlehem tell Naomi that the LORD is to be blessed because He has not left Naomi without someone to care for her and to look out for her. They see that this child is a miracle from God. God is the one who has provided for Naomi to have a kinsman. On the day the child was born, Naomi would, from that day on, have a kinsman that is a grandson; someone upon whom she could depend for the rest of her life. For a woman bereft of all save the love of a daughter-in-law, this was no small thing for God to have done for her.

That His Name May Be Famous In Israel.

Previously, the men of the city (the ten elders) had encouraged Boaz to do worthy deeds, so much so, that he would be famous for those deeds in Bethlehem. Now we hear this echoed by the women. They are saying, what God has done, is a great thing and because of it His name will be famous not only in Bethlehem but in the entire country of Israel. God wants to be known for His wonderful acts towards the children of men. He is to be praised for them, even as the women of Bethlehem have praised Him. God loves all men. He wants all men to hear of Him and to trust in Him so that He can be a blessing in their lives too.

Ruth 4:15 "And he shall be unto thee a

restorer of thy life, and a nourisher of thine old age: for thy daughter-in-law, which loveth thee which is better to thee than seven sons, hath borne him."

And He Shall Be Unto Thee A Restorer Of Thy Life,

The women are telling Naomi that this tiny baby will be the restorer of her life. They could mean that he will bring new life to her as only a baby can. As she watches him grow up, he will bring much joy to her. She will have much to look forward to as he takes his first steps and lisps her name.

All that is true but the women mean much more. The Hebrew word for restorer used here is shuwb and as well as restore it means to give back, to lead back, to refresh, to recall, and to cause to return. It is a movement back to the point of departure. We have seen this word many times. It is the same word for turn again and return. And while it is also true that Naomi has already returned, returned from Moab, the women are saying to her that this little baby will be the one who will finally bring her back to where she was before the disastrous move to Moab. This baby will bring her back to the person she was before. *He shall be unto thee a restorer of thy life.*

And A Nourisher Of Thine Old Age:

Old age, without a son to care for her and to provide for her, would have been bleak at best. Before the birth of this baby, that was all Naomi had to look forward to. Now with a grandson, so to speak, Naomi had a whole new old age to look forward to. Here was someone to sustain her and to care for and about her.

For Thy Daughter-In-Law, Which Loveth Thee

It is evident to everyone that Ruth still loves her mother-in-law dearly. Marriage to a very loving, understanding, compassionate, and well to do man, has not changed her and her feelings for Naomi. The birth of this baby is not only the result of the love of a man and a woman; it is also the result of the love of Ruth for Naomi.

Which Is Better To Thee Than Seven Sons,

If a woman had seven sons, surely she could count on being well cared for in her old age. The women may have picked the number arbitrarily but it is also the number associated with God; the perfect number. The women are saying that having Ruth is better than if she had had seven sons to depend upon in her old age.

Why have they said that? They are saying that Ruth is the best thing that could have ever happened in Naomi's life. They do not use Ruth's name because what they are talking about is relationship and their relationship is mother-in-law and daughter-in-law. Ruth, who was once "the Moabitess" is now referred to by the women of Bethlehem as daughter-in-law and praised to the highest degree.

Hath Borne Him.

The women are telling Naomi that all the credit for Naomi's wonderful prospects goes to Ruth. She is the one who bore this tiny person who would someday grow up to be the *restorer of thy life,* and *the nourisher of thine old age.* It is all because of the love of Ruth for her. Ruth *hath borne him.*

Ruth 4:16 "And Naomi took the child, and laid it in her bosom, and became nurse unto it."

And Naomi Took The Child,

Tears of joy must have filled Naomi's eyes when she first held this child. Even someone as pragmatic and practical as Naomi must have looked with awe at this tiny sleeping child. Truly a brand new life for her started at this moment as she held this brand new baby in her arms. Life was good and God, the author of all this goodness truly loved and cared for her.

And Laid It In Her Bosom,

Anyone who has held a newborn remembers the feelings of an indescribable and endearing awe. Naomi held the baby close to her heart. The word laid indicates that Naomi held him there for an extended time. It also indicates that the baby found rest with Naomi. Naomi obviously loved the baby for her loving Ruth's sake as well for his own precious sake.

And Became Nurse Unto It.

Nurse does not, in this case, mean to physically feed as it has come to mean in our culture. In England and many of the former Commonwealth countries, the term to nurse is still used today to indicate to hold or to cuddle. The Hebrew word for nurse is aman. It means to stand firm with the additional sense of trustworthiness and reliability. It also means to foster. It is easy to see Naomi as a reliable and firm loving grandmother who fosters this little boy in all he does. As the women predicted, no doubt in time he became her aman; a firm, reliable man who fostered Naomi in love.

> *Ruth 4:17 "And the women her neighbors gave it a name, saying, There is a son born to Naomi; and they called his name Obed: he is the father of Jesse, the father of David."*

And The Women Her Neighbors Gave It A Name,

The women of Bethlehem who lived nearby all started to call him the same name. They were friendly guileless women who were truly happy for their old friend Naomi.

Saying, There Is A Son Born To Naomi;

The neighborhood ladies were delighted for Naomi. They could see that her love for this little one was unusually tender. Naomi had carried the burden of having to be responsible for herself and Ruth. She had no husband or sons to be a moral or financial support. She once had the love and support of three men and too quickly that support was gone and she was bereft of all.

It had been overwhelmingly devastating but Naomi had not let it destroy her. She arose; she arose to every challenge that faced her and did not let her grief, despair, and disappointment destroy her. Neither did it destroy her faith in God. Yes, the LORD had allowed some very bitter situations in her life but she accepted responsibility and trusted in His love and care for her. She went forward with her life and left what once was, behind her.

This journey called life took her back to Bethlehem where her life had started with the LORD. She had to go back in order to go ahead and had found a secure future and it was all summed up in the tiny baby in her arms. He was not a son of her body or even a grandson but he might as well have been if being a son or grandson is measured in love.

And They Called His Name Obed:

Obed was not an unusual name in those days and is the name of several other men in the Scriptures. It means serving and is an apt name in regards to his future relationship to Naomi. The women knew that this baby served to give Naomi a new lease on life now in the present and would continue to do so in the future.

Obed would also serve God and pass on to his descendants all that he had gained from so godly a heritage.

He Is The Father Of Jesse, The Father Of David.

The women of Bethlehem had desired and prayed that this child would be famous in Israel. He became not only famous in Israel, but in every nation where the Word of God is read. Obed, who is by blood, only one quarter Israelite became the father of Jesse and the grandfather of the greatest king Israel ever had. He became the father of Jesse who was the father of King David.

> *Ruth 4:18 "Now these are the generations of of Pharez: Pharez begat Hezron,"*

Now These Are The Generations Of Pharez:

When we considered verse two in chapter one of the book of Ruth, we also looked at the following verses but it will be good to review them again in light of the whole book.

Just before Jacob died he called his sons together and prophesied over each of them.

> "And Jacob called unto his sons, and said, Gather yourselves together, that I may tell you that which shall befall you in the last days." Genesis 49:1

Jacob tells his sons what will happen over the centuries and millenniums to come. In the middle of his prophecy over Judah he says this:

> "The scepter shall not depart from Judah, nor a lawgiver from between his feet." Genesis 49:10

Here was given the prophecy of a kingly line among the descendants of Judah. Judah's first two sons died and then he had twin sons, the first born being named Pharez.

There is an interesting story about the birth of these twins and how Pharez got his name. When their mother Tamar went into labor, one of the little babies stuck out his hand. The midwife quickly tied a scarlet cord around his wrist so that they would know which baby was born first. The baby then drew back his hand and the other baby was actually born first. And the midwife said:

> "How hast thou broken forth? This breach be upon thee: therefore his name was called

Pharez." Genesis 38:29b

Pharez means breach or to break away. The midwife could not have known how appropriate this name would be for this tiny baby. From this point on, the promised kingly line would break away from any other descendants of Judah and follow this line of Pharez.

Pharez the son of Judah was the father of Hezron.

PAHREZ BEGAT HEZRON,

Hezron was the son of Pharez and the grandson of Judah. He was the eldest son of Pharez. Hezron means blooming. Hezron was a flower in the line of Judah. We see in him the promise of the blooming of this line. This line will bloom and holds the promise of full bloom when on that day the eternal scepter is held, by the king that is coming.

Ruth 4:19 "And Hezron begat Ram, and Ram begat Amminadab,"

AND HEZRON BEGAT RAM,

Ram, the son of Hezron and great grandson of Judah, was born in Egypt. His name means high. We see the coming king sitting in a high place.

And Ram Begat Amminadab,

We now come down to the great, great grandson of Judah named Amminadab. His name means people of liberty. When he was born, his parents were slaves in Egypt under cruel taskmasters but they had a hope, a vision, and a belief that someday God would free them from the hand of Pharaoh. It took a great deal of faith to name their little son Amminadab, people of liberty, but they held onto their belief that even in the darkest days of slavery God would make a way. With God, all things are possible and this they believed.

Ruth 4:20 "And Amminadab begat Nahshon, and Nahshon begat Salmon,"

And Amminadab Begat Nahshon,

Amminadab's name was a statement of belief by his parents. When his son was born he and his wife also demonstrated their faith by naming him Nahshon. Nahshon means rest or quiet. The LORD had promised them a land where they would find rest, that is, a place where they could live in peace and security even though for the foreseeable future and beyond the people of Israel would have to fight many battles before the Promised Land would be theirs.

Nahshon was part of the exodus from Egypt. Two years and two months after the exodus, God spoke to Moses and said He wanted all the men in each tribe over the age of twenty to be numbered. These were the men who would be able to go to war. God then gave the names of a man from each tribe to Moses. God appointed these men as leader of each tribe. For the tribe of Judah, He named Nahshon as the prince of the tribe of Judah, which numbered 74,600 men, who were able to fight. What an awesome responsibility.

How very incredible and humbling to be chosen by God Himself and entrusted with such enormous responsibility. Nahshon's sister, Elisheba married Aaron the brother of

Moses and Aaron was the high priest. This was a family of great faith and notable leadership qualities.

And Nahshon Begat Salmon,

To the prince of Judah was born a son and his name was Salmon. Salmon means strength or firmness. If ever there was a time for the people of Israel to stand firm in their faith and see the hand of the LORD it was now. As we have mentioned before, Salmon married Rahab who trusted in the LORD and hid the Israelite spies who were spying out Jericho.

Ruth 4:21 "And Salmon begat Boaz, and Boaz begat Obed,"

And Salmon Begat Boaz,

We have seen that this particular line of the family of Judah has been composed of godly leaders and we can now understand a little better why Boaz has become the man he is and the exemplary character he displays. God has a perfect plan for each life. These were men of great destiny. Since the number ten is the number of completeness, (refer back to the discussion of the number ten, chapter one, verse four) it is interesting that Boaz completes another tenth generation. From Adam to Noah there were ten generations. From Noah's son Shem to Abraham it is also ten generations. From Abraham's son Isaac to Boaz is the third set of ten generations. In each set of ten God had completed something and had started something new and it was always with a family. What is God beginning with this family?

And Boaz Begat Obed,

Obed means serving. We have seen that Obed will grow up to be a blessing to Naomi but his name also shows great faith on the part of his parents. Just as his ancestors before him, Boaz in allowing his son to be called Obed, shows that he and Ruth believed in the importance of serving the LORD. In the name of Obed we can just faintly hear the voice of his grandson predicting a time:

> "When the people are gathered together, and the kingdoms, to serve the LORD." Psalms 102:22

Looking ahead, there is a hint here that the coming king will also be a servant to his people.

> *Ruth 4:22 "And Obed begat Jesse, and Jesse begat David."*

And Obed Begat Jesse,

The grandson of Boaz and Ruth and the son of Obed was Jesse. Jesse means Jehovah exists which is a definitive statement about the firm belief of his parents. Jesse had eight sons. Many of these sons fought for Israel. The last time we hear of Jesse is when his son David is seeking refuge for him with the king of Moab. That is interesting since Jesse's grandmother Ruth was of course from Moab. It is possible that this further substantiates that Ruth was a princess of Moab.

And Jesse Begat David.

We have come to the end of book of Ruth but certainly not the end of the story. As we read on we find that David became the greatest king that Israel ever had and God promised David an eternal throne. His name means beloved and he was a person whom God called, "a man after His own heart." (I Samuel 13:14) On this expectant, forward looking note, and knowing that God wants to eternally bless His children, we come to the close of this lovely book of Ruth.

Epilogue

The book of Ruth ends with giving the name of Ruth's great-grandson David. Just as we know that much happened in history, leading up to the account we have of Ruth, there is much that happens after the end of her story. We do not know if Ruth lived long enough to hold the baby David on her lap and tell him of her coming to Bethlehem. He surely did hear the story though and we can hear in several of his Psalms the words of Boaz to Ruth when he talked to Ruth of the LORD, "under whose wings thou art come to trust." (The book of Ruth chapter two, verse 12) David used this quote in saying, "I will trust in the covert of thy wings." (Psalms 61:4 and see also 17:8, 36:7, and 57:1)

David was a man of much wisdom who loved the LORD. His beautiful songs, found in the book of Psalms will live on forever. The stories of his exploits and devotion to God will also live on forever. David eventually became King of Israel. He was not a perfect man but God called him a man after His own heart.

David's son was Solomon, the wisest man who ever lived. He was the king under whom Israel lived its golden age. He built the great Temple in Jerusalem. It has been called the most beautiful building ever built. God Himself designed the Temple. Solomon had two huge bronze pillars set up at the entrance of the Temple. It has been said that the artistry of casting such huge, beautiful bronze pillars has been lost and could not be duplicated today. Be that as it may, what is more interesting, is that Solomon named these two pillars. He named one Jachin which means God establishes. An eternal throne was promised to David. It has been established and one day a Son of David will reign forever. His throne will be set in the new Temple in Jerusalem, built without hands and He will reign forever and ever. Jachin, God has established.

The other pillar was named Boaz and has to be a tribute at least in part to Solomon's great, great, grandfather Boaz who took Ruth for his wife. Both the women of Bethlehem and the elders blessed their marriage. Upon the strength of this marriage and through this marriage, God used Boaz and Ruth to be the forebears of the eternal King of Kings.

From Obed, the son of Boaz and Ruth to the King of Kings is thirty generations. Three is the number of God. If three is multiplied times ten, which is the number of completion, we have thirty. God again worked through a family for a new beginning for the world for all mankind.

When God promised David an eternal throne it must have been hard for the future generations to believe it when, in later years, the people of Israel were taken into captivity and made slaves, once again, in a far off country. Their king was king no more. His kingdom was lost. The throne of David seemed to be lost irrevocably.

But God keeps His Word, His promises, and His plans, from before the beginning of time. They will be fulfilled. God had a plan, not only for the redemption of Ruth, but also for the redemption of all mankind. He would send another baby who was in direct line from Judah to whom the promise came of a scepter never departing from his family. The scepter promise passed through the marriage of Ruth and Boaz and on down to their great-grandson David to whom God promised an eternal kingdom that could not be lost.

Generations and generations passed, until another couple, (he was a descendant of David) had a little baby, also born in Bethlehem! They named Him Yeshua. This baby would grow up to be a kinsman redeemer too like his great, great…grandfather Boaz. He would grow up to be the King and of His Kingdom there would be no end. He came to redeem all mankind, to gain back what had been lost in the dawn of creation. God promised this baby would come, all the way back then.

How could a baby grow up to redeem all of lost innocence? Who could win the last great battle against death? Who could pay the price required of this kinsman-redeemer? Who could be the pure unspotted innocent lamb to be slain for the sins of the world? Who could be this great Messiah and Savior of mankind? He had to be of the tribe of Judah. He had to be in the kingly line of David. He had to be born in Bethlehem as foretold by the prophets. He had to be innocent (sinless) and He had to die. Without the shedding of blood there is no remission, no forgiveness of sin. Generation after generation of the children of Israel waited. And then one night the baby was born. Glory be to God in the Highest.

God had once more intervened on the behalf of all mankind. "For God so loved the world that He gave His only begotten Son that whosoever believeth in Him should not perish but have everlasting life." (John 3:16.)

God, through belief in His only begotten Son Yeshua (Jesus), wants you to have eternal life, and so much more. Trust Him. He loves you more than you can ever know. He wants to bless you; to be a blessing in your life right now. Talk to Him. Tell Him that you want Him to be your kinsman-redeemer. He has already paid the price for you with His life, His own blood was shed for you, the wonderfully unique individual that you are. Now is the time to decide to walk down that road just as Ruth did into a whole new life. If you have been away for a long time like Naomi was, now is the time to return. Confess your sin like Naomi did and walk all the way back to a new life, an abundant life that can only be found with Him.

You can read much more about all of this in the Bible. And although this is an epilogue, about what happened after the end of the book of Ruth, in truth there is no end to the story. Once you have opened your heart and life to the Lord Jesus, you too have become a vital part of this story. It will go on forever and ever.

I may be contacted by writing to:
P.O. Box 684
Westhampton, N.Y. 11977

Printed in the United States
36181LVS00003B/405